How *not* to ruin your small industry

S.J. PHANSALKAR

LIBRARY
SAINT PAUL COLLEGE
235 Marshall Avenue
St. Paul, Minnesota 55102

Response Books
A division of Sage Publications
NEW DELHI • THOUSAND OAKS • LONDON

Copyright © S.J. Phansalkar, 1996

All rights reserved. No portion of this book may be reproduced or utilised in any form or by any means, electronic or mechanical, including photocopying, recording, or any information storage or retrieval system, without permission in writing from the publisher.

First published in 1996 by

Response Books
A division of Sage Publications India Pvt Ltd
32 M-Block Market, Greater Kailash-I
New Delhi 110 048

Sage Publications Inc
2455 Teller Road
Thousand Oaks, California 91320

Sage Publications Ltd
6 Bonhill Street
London EC2A 4PU

Published by Tejeshwar Singh for Response Books, typeset by Print Line, New Delhi, and printed at Chaman Enterprises, Delhi

Library of Congress Cataloging-in-Publication Data

Phansalkar, S.J. (Sanjiv Janardan)
    How not to ruin your small industry / S.J. Phansalkar.
      p.   cm.
    1. Small business—Management.   I. Title
    HD62.7.P49   658.02′2—dc20   1996   96-16092

ISBN: 0-8039-9323-4 (US-hb)   81-7036-558-9 (India-hb)
            0-8039-9324-2 (US-pb)   81-7036-559-7 (India-pb)

Sage Production Editors: **Rakhshanda Jalil** and **Suchitra Vedant**

How *not* to ruin your small industry

About the Author

Dr S.J. Phansalkar runs his own management consultancy firm — Amol Management Consultants, Nagpur. Prior to this, he was on the Faculty of the Institute of Rural Management, Anand, during which time he completed the Fellow Programme in Management at the Indian Institute of Management, Ahmedabad. Dr Phansalkar has undertaken consulting assignments with various small-scale enterprises, and has published several research papers, newspaper articles and management cases.

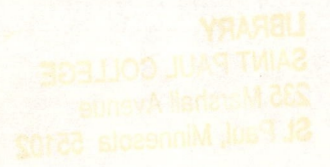

To
Bharati, my wife,
who encouraged me to write this book despite my tendency to make her a captive audience to my monologues on the subject.

And also to
the living spirit of enterprise
of lakhs of Indian entrepreneurs who give the country its vitality.

Contents

Preface   *9*

PART ONE: PRELUDE   *11*

1. Introduction to Small Business Management   *13*
2. Enterprises and Entrepreneurs: Then and Now   *21*

PART TWO: THE COMMON BLUNDERS   *33*

3. The Five Major Blunders   *37*
4. And the Three Lesser Blunders   *75*

PART THREE: MANAGING IT RIGHT   *103*

5. How Best to Manage Your Finances   *105*
6. Understanding and Managing Competition   *123*
7. A Matter of Style   *134*
8. Managing the Pangs of Growth   *143*
9. Your People Form the Core   *160*
10. So How Does One Get it Right?   *186*

Preface

This book is meant for all you busy and harried entrepreneurs who dream of becoming industrial giants. An understanding of one's problem is the first step towards solving it. This book will help small-industry owners such as you to understand the problems you are most likely to face. In several cases, I have indicated general ways of solving many of these problems, and where possible, avoiding them altogether.

I have attempted to write simply. Since the subject is not exactly elementary, there may be many statements which you may find slightly abstruse if you are not accustomed to reading an English text from cover to cover. Hopefully, these will be few, at least few enough to make you persevere.

This book is based on my interactions with numerous small-industry units. I was fortunate to get several opportunities to record my observations about their recurring problems and management styles. For a while I worked in a small industry which gave me first-hand experience of the problems. In this book I have attempted to analyse the various situations I have observed and encountered. For this reason I feel confident that you will find it of practical value.

There is another section of readers which this book addresses. They are those of you who may be contemplating setting up your own units and who could profit substantially by knowing what *not* to do. While I don't specifically aim to win accolades from my fellow management academics, I hope students and teachers of management will also use this book as a point of departure for their study of management processes in the small-industry sector.

I have tried to look at the business environment as it exists today, with its economic rent seeking and corruption. At the same time, I do not write with a reformist zeal, nor do I wish to push things under the carpet. In fact, many problems of the small industry originate in areas that conventional academic wisdom has preferred to keep a studied silence. To the extent that this realism brings in a certain earthiness to the book, it is intended.

Several persons including Profs Rajesh Agrawal, Samir Barua, B.P. Pethia, D.P. Mishra, M.S. Sriram and R. Srinivasan were kind enough to read earlier drafts of the manuscript and offer valuable comments. In addition, I discussed some of my ideas with several friends from the industry, which also gave me an opportunity to understand their ways of thinking. I am grateful for all their comments and help. Nevertheless, the views expressed in this book are my own.

S.J. Phansalkar

PART ONE

Prelude

After explaining my position in writing this book, I discuss the business environment and the impact of the new economic policy, on small industries in the country. All the policy changes have not taken effect, and therefore the impact is also not immediately visible. But the direction of change is for all to see and this is what I discuss in this section. In the context of the sweeping changes that have transformed completely the business opportunities available to the small industry, understanding and attempting to solve the management issues become even more important. This part stresses that for a substantial subset of the small industry, growth is not a matter of mere ambition but an imperative for survival.

Introduction to Small Business Management

The subject matter of this book

As my entrepreneur friends will undoubtedly tell me, there are many disagreeable things in the environment in which small industries operate. While not disputing this, I believe there are still many factors within the control of the entrepreneur himself. And how he handles those factors determines the destiny of his unit.

This book attempts to look at those areas of management which are in the hands of the entrepreneur. A close observation of the way a large number of small enterprises work reveals a pattern of decisions, small and big. I have attempted to dissect some of the major elements of this pattern. A detailed description and analysis of some of the commonly occurring problems in small-industry units show how they are related to this pattern of decision making. Detailed descriptions of a few small-industry units are introduced at many places to elaborate upon the genesis of these problems.

A detailed diagnostic list of questions is added at the end of the discussion of each of these problem areas to help the reader judge whether *his* unit suffers from the same problems or not. Finally, I have added a set of practical suggestions to diagnose, forecast and move towards finding a solution for these problems wherever necessary.

This book would remain incomplete without a discussion of the process and pains of growing which the enterprise and the entrepreneur must face. The process and its pitfalls form the next important component of this book. Again, desirable ways of managing this process are indicated.

However, there are many things which a reader will not find in this book. The reader will *not* find extracts of notifications of various departments pertaining to industrial development, or the rules framed by labour commissioners, excise and sales tax departments and so on.

I have refrained from making a detailed commentary on the history of government's policy on small industry, or debates on the definitions of small, cottage and tiny industry and their contributions to the national economy. This book does not even attempt a macro-economic analysis of the small-industry sector, its efficiency, equity and employment effects or its relative advantages or disadvantages in comparison with the big brother in Nariman Point and such other subjects dear to the economists. I prefer to remain in the realm of enterprise management.

What is small-industry management?

For the first time, through this book, I have introduced the question of defining what I mean by small. This discussion is largely for the benefit of those academically oriented readers who will insist on raising the issue of definition and delimitation of the topic. The entrepreneur may skip this section without missing much that will interest him.

Terms such as small (or for that matter, medium or large) industry are (*a*) relative, and (*b*) designed provisionally to help in the categorisation of industrial units for some practical purpose. Legal or quasi-legal definitions are designed for some practical purpose and hence subject to review and revision. Or else how can we explain why industries which employed a total capital of Rs 59 lakh were medium in 1990 but became small in 1991?

There *is* no firm, indisputable and yet defensible criterion for delimiting terms such as small or large industry. What we in India consider a giant, say a company such as Premier Automobiles Limited (PAL), is possibly unviably small in the eyes of a global player in the auto industry. The definitions of small and big industries become important for a pedagogic purpose only because they help us separate the problems and the possible solutions for the two categories. Obviously, the medium industry falls between two stools from this point of view. Let me explain.

If one makes *turnover* a basis of categorisation, things appear quite straightforward. But only for a moment. We find a one-man show of a 100 tonnes per day oil mill in Saurashtra crushing groundnuts reaching respectable sales turnover (about Rs 15 crore) and yet remaining essentially very simple to manage. Or a diamond-cutting unit in Surat for that matter. On the other hand, a turnkey project execution company dealing with, say, chemical industries will have a gruelling climb to reach this turnover, and yet be very difficult to manage.

If one were to hold investment in fixed assets as a basis of categorisation, again there would be problems. Many industries employing highly capital-intensive technologies will be, and for that very reason, quite small in terms of number of people employed and have a simple structure in managerial levels. On the other hand, industries employing relatively low capital could be involved in very complex businesses.

What I am driving at should now be evident. The only possible and defensible ground for categorisation for our purpose should be such that differentiating the management problems between categories is easy, and within categories pointless. I hold that the parameter for differentiating industries into small or large should be the amount of complexity involved in their management.

Complexity in the conventional sense is interpreted thus: a system is complex if it involves a large number of mutually interacting variables so that while predicting and manipulating it, it is necessary but nearly impossible to judge all the interrelationships among these variables. To give an example, the system of winds called monsoon is highly complex: even after careful selection the weather scientists have been unable to reduce the number of critical interacting variables in the monsoon system to less than sixteen. On the other hand, a city's water supply system is relatively simple, involving as it does relatively predictable and relatively independent variables like demand for domestic water consumption, behaviour of pipelines and supply in water resources.

Taking the concept to industries, the industrial unit (such as the vendor of RCC sleepers to a railway line) which makes a single product for one application in one market or a highly related group of products for similar applications to a very homogeneous market, is simple to manage. Or rather, simpler to manage than the industrial unit (such as say Hindustan Lever) which makes a large number of unrelated products for a variety of applications and in highly dissimilar markets. It is not surprising that the first instance is usually to be found among small industries and the second in large industries, though it is not necessary that this should always be the case.

Parameters such as sales turnover, investment in fixed assets and number of employees are simply surrogates for complexity. High sales turnover can come either by completely saturating a market in a small geographical area (such as the electricity boards or in consumer products such as Dinshaws, the unique ice-cream maker from Nagpur) or by selling in a widely distributed market such as most of the national consumer goods companies. The first involves complexity of managing intensive dependence and monopoly while the second obviously involves the complexity of logistics.

High capital investment in fixed assets obviously means the need to closely monitor the complex technical processes apart from the complexity of managing high operating leverage. Large employment is often caused by the number of interdependent tasks which have to be manually done for the final product to roll out and is by itself a cause of complexity which labour and industrial relations specialists know. Obviously, a large industrial unit is also more complex to manage.

By delimiting the sector of industrial activity by size as measured either by turnover, capital employed or employment, one is also delimiting by levels of complexity. And that is why there is this paradox: by definition the business of small industry management ought to be simple and yet seldom is!

Having said all this, let me make it clear that I have no quarrel with the legal or quasi-legal definitions of large, medium, small or tiny units as long as we know that these definitions are subject to change at the stroke of a bureaucrat's pen. For the sake of a rough-and-ready classification, let me say that this book is about management of industrial units which have invested less than

Rs 2 crore in fixed assets, have less than 100 employees on their rolls or on contract and have a sales turnover of less than Rs 10 crore. Thus, clearly Dhirubhai Ambani, Russi Mody and K.L. Chugh may not find this book interesting (not that they will ever read it, though I wish they did!).

Characteristics of small industries

The state of a nation's small industry is a barometer of the vibrancy of its economy at any given time. In our country, a third of all industrial output (and more if one were to ignore the public sector) and half of all the manufactured exports originate in the small sector. Japan owes its economic success not to Toyota and Mitsubishi but to the thousands of vendors on whose shoulders these enterprises stand. Then again, the small enterprises of today are the training and breeding grounds for the industrial giants of tomorrow. Finally, the small industrial sector in our country is also perhaps the most innovative one in terms of product design, management styles and logistics. Small, in this case, is beautiful.

The primary advantages of a small industrial unit come from low overheads, high flexibility and much faster decision making. Unfortunately, far too many such units operate in the commercial twilight zone. They take advantage of their anonymity in sidestepping regulatory and tax regimes. However, in the long run, dishonesty cannot be a source of competitive advantage. Witness, for example, the way the Surat powerloom industry reacted when the income-tax department launched a drive against it in 1986.

The disadvantages of small industrial units are equally obvious: absence of staying power, high production costs due to small scale of operations, inability to attract and retain highly skilled employees and qualified professional staff, and vulnerability to business fluctuations. Here again, the flip-side is the shadier side of management induced by anonymity: the need to spend a much larger part of their scanty resources and time in providing bribes and other forms of gratification to industrial buyers and to sundry regulatory officers, and an absence of the solid respectability granted to representatives of large industrial giants.

What is so special about managing a small industrial unit?

Particularly if, as I have argued, and I hope a few of my readers will get angry at my contention, it is less complex for managing? The special thing is to manage it in the absence or gross inadequacy of financial, technical or manpower strengths. And more importantly, managing the unit so that it remains small for as short a time as possible. While the child is pretty and vivacious, it must inevitably reach adulthood.

The theme of this book

Let me first reveal a sad personal observation: I was employed, after a high-profile MBA and an equally high-profile job, much to the opposition, amazement, ridicule of my colleagues and classmates, in a small industrial unit in 1979. The unit showed great potential of becoming an industrial giant. In 1979 the unit had crossed a turnover of a crore, which is equivalent in today's context of some 20 crore and was running profitably. I quit it for some collateral reasons. When I came across my former boss in 1994, his industrial unit still had a turnover of a crore! Believe me, when I returned home after meeting him, I was so depressed, I almost cried.

Well, there are entrepreneurs and industry owners who do not wish to grow at all. This absence of ambition may come from their fascination with some other walk of life: social work, education, sports or politics. They wish to keep their unit at a small and manageable size and use it only as a source of livelihood, not of self-fulfilment. Obviously, this book is not aimed at such people.

There are some people who are absolutely convinced that they are doing the best that can conceivably be done, that it is simply not possible to improve upon *their* management and that any one who suggests that it may be so lacks the necessary grasp over their business realities. To the extent that this claim is based on just plain complacence, I hope to make these people take a second look at their operations and their management style. But for those who have a closed mind on the subject, there is little point for them to read any further.

Thus, in brief, I am targeting this book at those industry owners who are open to ideas and who have a positive attitude towards their business. And also those who are in it for self-fulfilment. The aim of this book is to persuade the small-industry owner that it is in him to grow big, that growth is not an idle ambition but a positive imperative for survival and to show him how many of the most commonly adopted practices actually stunt him. I hope that at the end of perusing this book, I will be called upon for a greater personal dialogue by the reader-industrialist, for him to abuse and prove me wrong if he wishes, but hopefully also to help him grow bigger in his specific line of industrial activity.

The book is based on the premise that while prudent management along with chance factors lead to success in an industrial enterprise, failure can be made to order. It is difficult to give precise and infallible advice about how to succeed. The specific situation of an individual industry owner involves far too many details which need to be carefully understood and appreciated before such advice can be rendered. And even then, there will be uncontrollable factors whose influence can never be fully forecast. But given the will to undertake foolish acts of management, the most profitable industrial units can be ruined in no time. I am convinced that if any industrialist commits all the eight blunders which I have discussed in this book, his firm will definitely stagnate and most possibly become defunct soon. That is why I focus attention on guaranteed methods of courting disasters. The message should be clear: *Avoid all the eight blunders and there are very good chances that you have controlled the most important reasons of business failure.*

This book revolves primarily around eight common but almost stupid acts and decisions of management in small industries which keep the units stunted and struggling. It also provides you with symptoms and signs of recognising these mistakes. In the classical *Readers' Digest* style, if you can spot more than six of these mistakes in your unit, trust me, you had better do some thing fast if you want to remain in business for long. If you show between three and six of the symptoms, depending of course on which ones, there is some hope, though immediate action and changes are needed. Finally, if your management shows less than three of these mistakes then you show the wherewithal of a potential industrial giant.

Many people may get angry and ask me if I think I am the only wise man who knows that these are foolish management practices. No, I don't say I am. And if I am not the only sage, they will even more angrily ask, how come so many of the industrial units seem to act so needlessly? To tell you the truth, nothing is an absolute mistake or foolish act. It becomes so only in a given context. And as to why so many industrial units act that way, I just do not know. For the same reason, millions smoke though they know that it leads to cancer. And thousands of irritating Marutis driven by arrogant puppies still madly rush to overtake you even though they know that ninety nine per cent of road accidents occur during foolish acts of overtaking. So it is the individual's perception of risks and abilities to pull it through in the given situation which is wrong.

However, I hope you will agree that a man who is in the habit of incessantly smoking, driving at 90 kmph under the influence of alcohol, jumping traffic signals and also overtaking on busy highways, has only a few months left for him. That is why if an industrialist's perception is wrong in six of the eight cases, there is a genuine problem to be addressed. And if it is right in more than five cases, then it shows good judgement.

What follows

In the second chapter I digress a little, mainly with the intention of preparing a background for what is to follow. I deal there mainly with the sort of small-industry entrepreneur–manager whom we had in our country a few decades ago and the changes in that profile as seen now. I also deal with the challenges which confront the small-industry sector in the changed economic scenario. In the third and the fourth chapters (Part Two), I present the eight acts of omission and commission which are quite central to my theme. The subsequent chapters keep referring to them. Then in Part Three I have a chapter each on understanding and developing competitive strengths; the general business options which will more insistently force themselves upon the entrepreneurs; key areas of financial management and the processes and pangs of growth. Part Two warrants the most careful and critical reading followed by an enquiry into one's own operations.

2

Enterprises and Entrepreneurs: Then and Now

Emergence of small industry in India

In traditional India, business activity was of two basic types: the craft of the artisans, and trade-cum-money-lending activities of the mercantile capitalists. In the urban setting, business meant mainly trading. Often minimal processing of the traded commodity, usually restricted to dividing in smaller lots, packaging and so on was carried on as an add-on activity. Business still does mean largely this in the industrial backwaters of modern India in places such as Nagpur, Patna and Cuttack. Such places are busy commercial centres, but not industrial belts. The manufacturing activity was concentrated in a few pockets. Elsewhere, it focused on simple products for urban living.

The directly home-service-oriented manufacturers—the furniture maker, the grill and gates fabricator, the baker and others to be found in profusion—were more like overgrown artisans' workshops rather than factories. From this background the Indian industry of today emerged over a few decades, through several not very significant phases of transition.

The most frequent pioneers in the industrial fields were the mercantile capitalists: the traditional *banias* of north India, whether *marwaris* from Rajasthan, *lalas* from UP and Haryana or their equivalent communities from other parts of the country such as the *kayasthas* from Bengal, the *chettiars* from Tamil Nadu and the *shahs* from Gujarat. The only exception to this broad trend were the enterprising Sikhs from the north and the Patels from Gujarat. But by and large, the traditional trading communities dominated. This dominantly mercantile-capitalist background carried its own set of attitudes into the industry, such as preoccupation with immediate and quick profits, tendency to save on costs for non-immediate gains, speculation on price-rise and extreme conservatism regarding fixed investments.

The prevailing ethos too reinforced this set of attitudes. Almost till the end of the seventies, the Indian economy was shortage ridden and hamstrung by stifling controls. In this atmosphere, rent-seeking rather than manufacturing abilities produced more profits, and it made sense to concentrate on that. Had I been in business then, I would have done exactly that.

To make good profits, the laundry soap manufacturer (an activity long reserved for the small sector) did not really have to make soap. He had to ingratiate the man from SSIDC (Small Scale Industries Development Corporation) to give him an allocation of caustic soda and then simply sell it in the black market. (And with marginal tax rates upwards of 75 per cent, it made more sense to earn one hundred rupees in black money rather than three hundred in white.) The same was true with any one who needed steel: you could claim that you are a fabricator in the SS category, have steel allotted and sell it off at a profit. And so it went in many other industries. (The government eventually got wise to this business and introduced 'checks and balances' in the form of 'Actual User' certificates; it is a different story that these checks and balances became [bearer] cheques and [unearned bank] balances!)

A 'genuine manufacturer' who concentrated on high quality manufacture was considered an exception. This scarcity of good manufactured products again led to a black market in *their product!* (I remember my family being willing to pay a premium on Dalda by Hindustan Lever rather than buying 'any other *faltu dalda*'!)

This permit-quota-ration raj also brought in another set of entrepreneurs: the 'brother and son-in-law' set. Many a worthy minister and even a lesser MP used his influence to get his brother, brother-in-law, nephew or some such relation an industrial licence, a certificate from the DGTD (Director General of

Technical Development) or other form of scarce authorisation for starting an industrial undertaking. Many preferred rent seeking of various kinds to honest hard work. Some, of course, turned out to be very capable and have become very respectable industrialists today. The ethos certainly permitted rent seeking on a massive scale if you happened to be well connected.

The entrepreneurs of the nineties

The transition to today's entrepreneurs really began in the mid-eighties. From the days of the Dagli Committee report onwards, controls started loosening. After the finance ministership of V.P. Singh, shortages started reducing. These steps gained momentum after 1991, vastly reducing the scope for rent seeking. Today much of the small industry has started working towards producing quality goods acceptable to the consumers to earn its profits.

The profile of the entrepreneur too began changing in the eighties. More and more entrepreneurs today are professionally or technically trained and qualified people. They are also street-smart and literate. They see where the economy is going and they intend to grab their share of the growth. They are also far more modern in outlook than their predecessors were. They do not get shocked at the thought of buying expensive gadgets for superior technology and management quality. Computers, for example, are now more or less accepted as an indispensable part of the tools of their trade.

The entrepreneurs today try and keep abreast of what is happening in their industry in terms of products, technology and markets. They do not mind the expense involved in attending trade fairs, exhibitions, seminars and workshops for this purpose. In personal life, too, they present a modern outlook. Most of them now wish to associate with professionally trained people in and around their operations. The ubiquitous *munim* and the *sahab ka aadmi* are getting replaced by professionals whose contribution is valued more in terms of competence than mere slavish loyalty.

It is this new class of entrepreneurs on whom the country can place hopes of a great industrial resurgence. This entrepreneur is fairly competent with the technical side of his industry. He understands the processes involved in production and the technical ways of increasing process efficiency. He is also a good judge of what is needed for qualitative improvement in his product as well as the need to put these improvements into effect.

His problem, unfortunately, is that he too is falling a victim to the short cuts permitted by the ethos. The regulator of quality, safety and fiscal levies is still eminently available for purchase for thirty pieces of silver. And rather than following the straight and sure path of solid growth, it is still very tempting to cut corners wherever one can to reach the top quickly. The danger that in cutting corners continuously one may simply go round in circles is often not realised. Many an entrepreneur is still tempted to do the quick and the dirty thing rather than be straight and good. And he feels that he knows all the ropes and all the right people. And worse still, he feels that even if he does not, a middleman going under the respectable sounding title of a consultant will help him pull the necessary strings. From the ethos of the mercantile capitalists, we may be moving towards the more disagreeable phase of industrial revolution: that of the brazen buccaneer.

This sort of entrepreneur is often not well-versed in the complex processes of growth management and of a growing organisation. That is mainly because he has had no occasion to learn about such things. The first flush of success brings with it a justifiable pride in one's achievement. This pride has the danger of becoming a feeling of know-all arrogance. That, in turn, leads to a sort of contempt for all supportive staff and others in the task environment.

It is very easy to hog all the credit for success. After all, has the entrepreneur not sacrificed comforts in his personal life and invested long working hours in his business? Has he not taken financial risks when others were getting their monthly pay cheques? Has he not burnt the midnight oil during busy times when all his staff wanted to run away at five-thirty? Of course he has, and he therefore must get the credit for the success and the sweet things that go with it.

Such self-adulation naturally makes it easy to forget that most of what one has achieved has to do with the contribution of others: the workers, the salesmen, the bankers and so on. This realisation is the key to managing the relationships with all the contributing and supporting individuals and organisations—something that is indispensable to good general management. In effect, many an entrepreneur fails to become a good general manager.

The chief problem of transition from the status of an entrepreneur to that of a general manager or CEO, call it what you wish, is the inability to give up control. The need for control arises out of an intense feeling of proprietary ownership for the machines, the factory, the product, the technology and the way of doing things in general. The art of delegation, so necessary if the enterprise is to grow in size and the entrepreneur in stature, can be mastered only when this excessive control orientation is curbed. And growth is absolutely essential in the changed context as I shall presently argue.

The New Economic Policy and small industries

At least four elements of the economic policy adopted by the Government of India since 1991 vitally affect the small industry. They are:

- Substantial dereservation of items hitherto reserved for the small sector;
- Wholesale freeing of markets for powerful and cash-rich organisations including multinationals;
- Massive diminution in the role of the public sector in the scheme of things; and
- The near-end of the permit-quota or dual price regimes in most of the industrial commodities as well as scarce inputs such as power and credit.

Simultaneously, there has been a definite trend towards greater consumer awareness and popularity of convenience goods which has caused much greater branding and image creation in products which were hitherto traded without any fanfare. The result of these GOI policies and subsequent market trends is that the happy days for the small industry have gone forever. The small industry must now learn to fend for itself. This it must do by growing in size and in strength. The thrust of this chapter is precisely that growth is a prerequisite if the small industrial unit wishes to survive in the changing scenario.

This growth should be in terms of

- Size to reap the advantages of scale
- Reach to diversify market risks
- Range to fully exploit synergies across products and services and greater claim in managing the supply chains of the buyer.

The most important facet of growth will have to be a forced change in the mindset of the entrepreneur—from that of a rent- seeking small fly-by-night operator to a giant in the making. The message is: Grow or Go!

Perhaps many a small entrepreneur was not even aware of the reservation policy. That, however, is immaterial; the large industry was prevented from entering, for whatever reason, and that helped the small fellow any way. No more. Most of the products hitherto reserved for the small sector will get increasingly branded and marketed in an organised manner. Thus the markets for items reserved for the small sector, say ordinary electric motors of small power, will become increasingly dominated by products branded and marketed by a strong and powerful marketing agency. This trend has, of course, been very strongly evident in electric goods for a long time. There are also several other products, such as wheat and gram flour, spices and condiments, curry powders, instant food mixes, pickles and papad—all products reserved for the small sector—which are showing this trend.

What one will see is the emergence of national brands in a majority of such products; some are already there, others will emerge. But the production base will have to be much larger than permitted in the small sector. So one or probably both of these will happen: the brand owner will keep floating more and more units in the small scale duplicating production facilities, or if dereservation is not complete soon enough, then he will seek to lease out facilities of other small units or get them to pack under his brand.

There will be consolidation and emergence of fewer and relatively stronger brands in most of the product categories, whether made and marketed in India by Indian firms in the small sector or made by the small sector and marketed by a large-sector intermediary. The lure of this burgeoning Indian middle class is bringing in consumer marketers of MNC origins in droves and they are bound to put pressure for complete dereservation soon. Even that will mean a great amount of contract manufacture, most likely on facilities owned by small-scale industries but under the overall supervision of the MNCs, as is happening in the bottled soft drink industry.

Naturally, certain ideological compulsions, the 'sacred cows' and social pressures will force the government to avoid complete product dereservation. Thus, the products made by units registered with the Khadi Village Industries Corporation (KVIC) will continue to enjoy protection of reservation for quite some time, as the KVIC is a sacred cow. Similarly, many subsidies and favoured treatments will continue, such as the subsidy for handloom units. But the trend is towards greater freedom of market and access to market players irrespective of size. The small sector obviously has to take notice and wake up.

In the case of many products, there may be a greater advantage for a local player. He may continue to remain small. For example, while national players in the grill and gate fabrication units will emerge sooner or later, the ironsmith round the corner has obvious advantages of being local. For that matter with the best of branding and marketing, a Godrej can never hope to drive small steel office and domestic furniture makers out of business because of the massive disadvantages in transporting fabricated stuff compared to transporting a 20 gauge ms plate. Similarly, products needed for building construction such as sand, lime or bricks do not appear in the immediate possibility of branding, though construction itself is getting more and more corporatised.

However, aside from such products giving scope for transportation advantages for the small sector, removal of unit size restriction on production/marketing of a whole lot of other items will essentially cause a trend of emergence of fewer, more organised brands controlled by larger and stronger organisations. The small-industry owner engaged in the manufacture of these will have to either become a vendor to one of these marketers (and hence need to understand the trick of being a good vendor without being exploited) or join hands with many of its kind and offer a brand of its own. Only in a few products which offer distinct advantages of location specificity will the original situation of faceless manufacture and marketing continue.

The lesson is clear: many small industries will have to learn the skills of marketing in order to compete with much larger organisations. And that may mean that they will have to develop product features which give them a niche, and/or develop and monopolistically access segments of market and service them to prevent entry of the giants.

Now let me focus at the remaining two changes in government policies. They are:

- The loss of importance and change in policy towards public sector units; and
- The substantial reduction in controls and subsidies on raw materials and inputs such as credit.

In my view both tend to cut at the very root of those small-scale units which existed merely on account of possibilities of rents arising out of such things as price preferences, controls and subsidies.

If, as is the case now, small and large units both have to buy steel at the same price and there is no shortage, obviously the inefficient and high-cost small units will eventually disappear. And it would be a good thing too for it will make for a cleaner public life. The reduction in the profile of the public sector unit will mean a greater challenge to the small industry but that will not be an unmixed calamity.

In many an industrial backwater, small industry existed merely as a set of vendors and service units for the nearby public sector undertakings (PSUs). The PSUs were seldom bothered with their financial performance. Quite a few were dens of corruption. Apart from the fact that dubious business dealings became more important than good quality–cost parameters in winning orders from them, there was a major problem in this sort of situation. The small units were often solely dependent on the PSU buyer. As the fortunes of that buyer changed, the small-industry vendor simply went out of business. When the PSU delayed payments, the supplier's liquidity was clogged.

The situation was not sustainable any way. The current drive towards the financial viability of PSUs and cutting of budgetary support to them were heralded as a welcome end to this era. Those small industries which have developed alternate applications of processes and machines usually used for making products for public-sector buyers will survive. Others who failed to do this will go under, with little cause for communal regret.

The onslaught of established international brands in the consumer sector and the withdrawal of crutches in the form of preferential treatments (pricing and allocation of critical commodities, preferred buying from small suppliers and price preference regimes) by public sector and parastatal organisations will thus deal a body blow to many a small industry. No wonder, the government too is worried about the impact of globalisation on small industries. But the juggernaut has been set in motion and is perhaps irreversible.

Still, there are many options available for the small industry. Consolidation, a highly desirable thing any way, is one such option for it offers the twin advantages of improving production efficiency and enhancing marketing strengths. Some of the other options are deliberate choice of high-profile growth by seeking market funds for financing expansion, incorporation into an existing large unit, joint venture with a foreign operator, being bought over by some one, etc. We will have occasion to look at these in greater detail later.

Recent changes in environment

It is clearly impossible for a very large number of small industrial units to engage in the sustained export of goods on their own for a long period of time. Such a thing is possible only for a certain class of industry, such as the ready-made garment sector, the artifacts and handicrafts units, the spices and condiments sector, and the gems and jewelry sector. By and large, others will have to enter into long-term arrangements with global players who are looking for cheap suppliers of components and modules of their products. Such a search for sourcing partners has already begun in a big way by Japanese industries. A decade or so ago, they began sourcing of components and parts in Taiwan and Korea. As these countries too have become high-labour-cost economies, they are looking towards India for identifying partners for sourcing their requirements. This presents a major breakthrough for the Indian small industry.

Then there are some other recent changes which seriously affect the small entrepreneur. The first is the new convention on intellectual property rights under the WTO framework. India has agreed in principle to change over from mere process patenting to product patents. That will mean 'me-too' products using stolen technology and cheap 'as-good' imitations of top-line consumer products, will no longer be as lucrative as before. The danger of legal actions with expensive penalties being imposed for violations will become increasingly real.

The second change in this line is the environment issue in which even the Indian judiciary is taking an increasingly active interest. Courts have already ordered closure of hundreds of small and medium units in western India for failure to address pollution matters. The *hafta* will no longer take care of these 'minor irritants' if the Courts are repeatedly approached by environmental activists. So investments in pollution control measures will become necessary for the small enterprises as well.

The third is the issue pertaining to employment of child labour. That hurts many of the craft-based small industries. The light engineering and other such industries hire no child labour but the carpet, matchbox and fire-cracker units do. So wherever the employment of child labour has been customary, the effect will be noticeable. In this as well as the environment issue, the small industry has to face increasingly vocal activist groups which find a sympathetic ear in the Courts, making the bureaucracy relatively toothless.

Thus globalisation of the Indian economy, while being a massive threat to much of the small sector in the short run, also presents a great new opportunity. There is no doubt that in many respects the Indian economy offers unique advantages to an industrialist who wishes to be or is associated with a great global player. The first such advantage is the presence of very large, solvent and growing domestic market which, at least for the moment, is not too choosy in terms of quality. Such a large market provides depth, stability and a solid foundation to some one who has his eye on the global market.

The second advantage is the availability of very cheap engineering manpower, much cheaper than anywhere in the world. This provides for an endless sea of resources and opportunities for systematic technology experimentation, at a cost never possible any where else in the world.

The third advantage is the abundance of an undoubtedly cheap labour force, one that will only become easier to manage with the passage of time. But there is a flip-side to this. The realisation that ultra labour-friendly laws are deterring investments in the country is increasingly gaining ground.

Next, our country is so well blessed with such a wide range of primary produce, of which we have not exploited even one-fiftieth.

Finally, there is a very export-friendly regime at the moment, and by all indications the orientations are unlikely to change for some time to come. The constraints are mainly of the psychological kind on the part of the industrialists. A get-rich-quick kind of impatience and greedy and myopic outlook of the industry owners tends to muzzle the truly massive but long-term possibilities.

One has to realise that to succeed in the global market, an industrial unit has to satisfy three prerequisites:

- It must have the patience and the preparedness to undertake painstaking improvement in the quality of its products;
- It must be prepared to look at global operations as a permanent part of its operations, not merely as an add-on for the sake of social legitimacy or export incentives and finally;
- It must invest time and managerial resources in developing relationships of a durable nature with potential intermediaries and buyers in the national as well as global markets.

PART TWO

The Common Blunders

I am writing this book for obviously those who would like their unit to remain healthy and to grow into an industrial giant one day in the not-too-distant future. Therefore, for those readers who actually yearn for 'voluntary sickness' for their industrial units (for whatever unworthy reasons), what follows is more or less a practical recipe for making the unit sick.

In the first chapter, I had stated that it is common knowledge that the acts of commission and omission I shall presently mention are wrong and almost stupid. I had then asked how come entrepreneurs commit them on such a large scale, or why are these acts so popular. I pretended that I did not know and compared this prevalence with that of smoking or overtaking on busy highways.

I was being provocative and a bit naughty. There are solid reasons why some of these mistakes *appear* to be the right thing to do at the time of crisis. Many times there are professional advisers who tell you to commit these blunders. The ethos sometimes demands wrong managerial action. It needs an exceptional level of managerial sagacity to see through the clutter, judge where your long-term interest lies. Common sense is perhaps a better guide and is definitely more generously distributed than sagacity.

Also, as I had hinted earlier, unrealistic government policies regarding pricing, taxation, product reservation, labour laws, etc., practically encourage dishonesty and falsehood.

It was and still is profitable for a unit to claim it has a turnover of, say, only half a crore of rupees when in fact it has a turnover of seventy lakh rupees, as then excise duty is chargeable and the customers, who are similarly enmeshed in a web of fiction and falsehood for their own reasons, turn away to other suppliers to avoid the paperwork of MODVAT. (I merely illustrate my point, I do not know nor do I care at what sales turnover level a unit has to pay excise duties. The Finance Ministry keeps changing it.) Another trick is to split the unit in two when you reach an employment size of 45 so that you won't have to start a canteen or some such benefit. With scores of regulatory acts and rules, each putting a limit for change of categories at a different level than the other, this sort of a logic for perpetually living in a world of falsehood is an ever-present reality.

Then there is always the lure of the coin, the colour of money becoming fast irrelevant with greater 'openness' in the investment climate. I do not wish to speak the holier-than-thou language. Not having been presented an opportunity to amass a fortune does not make me a saint. The point is, the lure of the coin also encourages myopic decisions.

The third common rationalisation is the inevitable time gap between the realisation of the opportunity (or its creation by enterprising efforts) and the development of financial and organisational muscle to exploit it effectively. Take the following scenario: The product one is making clicks, the market appears large, or the prices of raw materials suddenly turn favourable, but the bank does not give extra credit limit. The term lending institution drags its feet. In such circumstances, is one to give up the opportunity? Or should one resort to adventurous financing, repeating to all those who advise caution that there is no gain where there is no risk? This sort of adventurous financing can some-times be based on miscalculation; therefore it backfires. What remains is the prosaic accounting and financial record based on which an external analyst like me comments, 'Ha! Blunder number 2 (or 3 or 4)'.

Unfortunately, for even the best of entrepreneurs, the time gap between opportunities and proven strength will never be long enough. In fact, for the good entrepreneur, there will always be far more opportunities than his strengths permit him to grab. Nor will all the calculations in all these adventurous decisions be always right. So there will always be the possibility of these mistakes occurring.

Some of the blunders are, however, at times completely without any justification or charitable rationalisations of the above kind. I shall certainly point out the blunders of this kind in the next two chapters.

What I propose to do is the following: For each one of these blunders, I shall present, completely disguised but extremely realistic, examples of entrepreneurs and enterprises which I have observed. I shall also indicate the rationale or the expressed reasoning behind these decisions. I shall put forth the alternatives which the concerned entrepreneurs had at the time. Then I shall submit why I consider a particular kind of decision as myopic and the rough description of the stage at which and the time frame in which it will affect the entrepreneur. I shall then list a set of questions which should help you judge whether you are committing that blunder as well as provide the options to avoid it and the cost of those options.

A disclaimer

In order to ensure complete anonymity of the real-life cases involved, I had referred to all entrepreneurs as Vishwakarma, all products as STUFF, all private sector industrial buyers of the Vishwakarma as COMPANY, all products of the COMPANY as PRODUCT, all public sector buyers of the Vishwakarma as NIGAM, all lending banks as BANK, all authorities as DEPARTMENT, and places as SMALL or LARGE TOWNS in my first draft. I found that this detracted from the readability. Now I am using real-sounding names. However, it should be remembered that any resemblance between the actions attributed to a name and actions actually committed by the worthy person/corporate body of that very name is miraculously coincidental.

3

The Five Major Blunders

BLUNDER 1: Exclusive or excessive dependence on one buyer

Description of the case

Sharma is a good friend. After finishing his engineering degree from a reputed college from Rajgarh, he went on to do his Master's from an internationally renowned institute in Bombay. Later, he worked for a big COMPANY called General Machines Ltd as an engineer supervising production. His father encouraged him to set up a small industry in Rajgarh where he eventually decided to settle down. Sharma started the industry in 1984, in his father's backyard. He started out by making some specialised relays for Hindustan Corporation.

The Service Department in charge of Hindustan Corporation had set up a large number of operating units in many towns with population exceeding five lakh all over India. All of them had to buy some relays every year. Sharma soon hired Verma, a friend of his. Later they became partners. Sharma and Verma worked very hard. Sharma went around meeting the officers of the Corporation in all the towns to 'persuade' them to buy his relays. This persuasion took time and was often 'expensive'.

Given their typical working style, the officers at the Corporation offices all over the country tended to place their order for the relays only in February/March. The particular technical specifications of the sort of relays needed at a particular branch were not specified in advance, and the particular relay had to be designed, developed and delivered to the branch in just under a fortnight or at the most a month.

Sharma had to hire a number of engineers for doing this design job. While the Corporation was at times very keen to buy the relays from him and price was never very much a negotiated matter any way (as it was technically needed urgently), the Corporation was very erratic in its payments. This was because the Corporation depended on sanctions from the Service Department for both buying as well as paying the bills. The erratic payment pattern resulted in Sharma's sundry debtors becoming almost as large as the total sales figure in a given year.

Owing to the unpredictable nature of the technical specifications, Sharma could not plan properly for buying the raw materials and parts. This resulted in massive and largely useless inventory. Sharma could not say when the stock on hand would be used. By 1994, he had reached a sales turnover of Rs 160 lakh, all of which came from branches of the Corporation from various parts of the country.

In 1994 the Service Department announced its plans to make these branches responsible for their financial viability. It had also mooted privatisation of a lot of its services, inviting multinational companies to do the same work.

The year 1995 saw Sharma's factory showing a drop in demand from Rs 169 lakh in the previous year to some Rs 95 lakh. He was deeply worried about what might happen to his unit. He had about sixty people on roll, of whom over a dozen were engineers. His firm had no experience of making any thing on a large scale to reduce the costs by proper purchases, nor developed systems and procedures of managing employee time, productivity or item inventories. And now the Corporation branches were going to keep on reducing their orders for the relays.

What is the entrepreneur's rationale?

Excessive or exclusive dependence on one buyer is a blunder which a very large number of entrepreneurs commit. In fact, it is so prevalent that many will not even notice it. Surely you would agree that such complete dependence as this (100 per cent sales to the same sort of buyer units of one Corporation) is not a wise thing. Why, then, did Sharma do it? His logic was that the orders were so easy to handle and that the Corporation was always in desperate need for the supplies. The officers he dealt with were highly bureaucratic and quite bad planners of their purchases or maintainers of their machines.

When any machine broke down, they would rush around for the relay. And since Sharma was about the only manufacturer of that kind of relay, he was always given the orders at attractive prices. The investments which Sharma made in initially 'persuading' these officials were very important. Besides, the Corporation presented such an image of a stable and large buyer that there appeared no harm in depending exclusively on it. Yes, the Corporation did pay very late, but it was like a government deal, the money was safe and since he could always include the interest on the blocked money and much more in the initial price itself, it really did not hurt him.

Perhaps he should have also done a bit of business with some other buyers on the side while ripping the Corporation, but he never had any time to concentrate on the smaller fry.... After all, there were so many things to do and only two of them to do it all.

How much of this sounds like good reasoning and how much as pure self-delusion is for you to judge.

Why is this a blunder?

The small industry does not have a monopoly to this sort of blunder. This also happens to some large industry units. See for example the case of a large company given in Box 3.1.

This one blunder causes more business failures in the small sector than any other. The failures can, at times, be tragic, as in the case of Vidarbha in the last decade.

An auto manufacturer agreed to set up a manufacturing plant in a small town in Vidarbha. The Government of Maharashtra agreed to give it some very attractive backward-area benefits only if it created and supported ancillary units. So it went about attracting entrepreneurs of the more naive kind, promising them orders for auto components. Some 35 ancillary units were set up in Vidarbha. Most of them were started by first-generation entrepreneurs, goaded and beguiled by a combination of the local SSIDC and the auto manufacturer. Many of them, unfortunate creatures, had given up secure jobs, pawned wife's gold and mortgaged houses to set up their units. After all, if an auto giant promises steady orders per month to you, your business is safe, or so they thought.

BOX 3.1
A case of exclusive dependence on one buyer

Back in the sixties, an MNC called Guest.Keen and Williams (GKW) used to have over 80 per cent of its business from the Indian Railways. The company was a subsidiary of Guest Keen and Norton of UK. It specialised in things such as safety pins and fasteners. But the bulk of its business came from the Railways. In 1965, the country went on a war with Pakistan, and in 1966 the rupee was devalued. In the aftermath, the Railways cut back their orders very substantially. That was also the period characterised by the dependence of the Indian economy on the monsoon, its relative isolation from world markets, strong economic fetters on starting, continuing and even discontinuing industrial activity and stifling controls on all foreign trade. The Railways took years to resume their pre-1965 level of buying and GKW had very few alternative buyers to provide the same level of business.

The results for GKW were traumatic. The company went in such a spin it took them almost a decade to fully recover; and that too after significantly diversifying its product line. It began manufacturing Cold Rolled Grain Oriented Steel in the country, while it had only imported from GKN till then. GKW has since then been progressively reducing its dependence on the Railways.

About Rs 100 crore were paid out as subsidy in various forms. The auto giant did not spend even a crore on materials from the so-called ancillaries. Thirty-one of them have folded up by now. The three or four who survive were those who had installed general-purpose machines on which job works of different kinds could be undertaken.

Exclusive or excessive dependence on one buyer is obviously not a very healthy thing to do. Many people understand this and are, therefore, naturally wary of falling in its traps. But there are also a lot of people who actually indulge in this kind of self-induced and almost foolish myopia. Dependence on the PSU is only one part of it. It is not an absolute error, however. The key mistake is to create excessive *asset specificity* without firm and long-term contracts which use specific assets.

Asset specificity refers to the creation of machinery, skills and facilities which can be used only in one particular way and for one particular purpose. The positive description of asset specificity is 'dedicated' facilities. The trouble arises only when the dedication is one way.

Most businessmen cry foul when presented with the option of creating asset specificity at their own expenditure. I can think of a perfect example of earthy common sense shown by the truck driver-owners from Punjab. One MNC milk processing giant operating from a small town in Punjab wished to hire trucks for bringing milk from the villages. Their transportation whiz-kid told them that if milk cans could be arranged in two or three tiers, using metal or wooden structural frames for holding the upper layers, the transportation cost per litre would diminish sizeably. They floated tenders asking for rates on an annual basis with and without these structural arrangements on the truck bodies.

The results were remarkable: if an ordinary truck was to be used, then on an annual contract the truckers were happy with only Rs 1.80 per km. (I am talking of a situation in the early eighties.) If the company wanted trucks with frames for three-tier can holding, the rates were Rs 6 per km. And the company was asked to:

- Spend the money on converting the bodies; and
- Give a guarantee of minimum mileage per day.

Obviously, with frames for holding three tiers of milk cans filled in the trucks, nothing else could be transported in the bodies and there would be complete asset specificity. In other words, the truckers wanted a lot of assurance in return.

In fact, all ancillarisation is problematic from the point of view of the one who is being ancillarised. And 'vendor development' is an even greater danger for him! Any small industry which is selling only to one company becomes a virtual slave to it. While they sing the praises of the Just-in-Time (JIT) systems, efficient vendor-relation management and the lot in their five-star training workshops, many large Indian companies are still wholly untrustworthy from the point of the ancillary. After all, the auto giant of the Vidarbha case cannot change his soul in a mere decade! If the buyer is a rogue, as buyers sometimes turn out to be, the ancillary is doomed.

The ancillarisation contract must be accompanied, if the ancillary is to feel safe, by a counter-guarantee that the buyer will not buy the agreed item from more than the agreed list of parties and will buy at least a certain quantity per month. Otherwise the ancillary is better off remaining an operator on the spot contract only.

The solution to this one-sided dependence is to create a situation of *mutual dependence*, that is, don't let the buyer have everything his own way all the time. Only then will he behave.

What alternatives did Sharma have?

Obviously, the real alternative to exclusive or excessive dependence on one buyer is simple: Do not depend on one buyer. Sounds simple, does it not? How could Sharma have avoided a major setback?

Sharma could have systematically ensured that no more than half the sales were to the branches of the Corporation. This could only be done in two ways. One was to systematically develop alternate products using the same machines and skills as needed for the original relays, for other buyers. The second way was to develop alternate markets for the same relays. In other words, risk of the volume of sales or the realised price turning sour had to be reduced by developing alternative markets which are similar to the original buyer.

This is called simple market-risk diversification. Sharma sold his relays to the Corporation, controlled by the Service Department, obviously operating in a near-monopolistic situation. This is very similar to several corporate diversifications, including that of GKW Ltd., a case discussed in Box 3.1. GKW could possibly not find alternate buyers for products meant for the Railways, so what they must have done was to introduce new products.

In case of less severe buyer concentration, where at least a few other buyers exist (such as the case of the auto ancillaries described earlier), the problem could be tackled by the ancillary units approaching players in the auto industry other than the one in Vidarbha for the components. In fact, in ordinary advertisements of most auto ancillaries you will see virtually *all* Indian auto makers listed as their buyers!

In effect, market risk is diluted by selling in many rather than only one market, to many buyers rather than only one buyer and dealing with many rather than only one product. But a vast majority of small industries are single-product firms. For them, diversification must be done across buyers. Examples of typical diversification by buyers which I am familiar with are: Original equipment manufacturers (OEMs) as well as replacement segments for most of the industrial component makers (e.g., selling to *motor manufacturers* as well as to rewinders in the case of winding wire), *household* and *institutional* in case of food industry, and *city* investors as well as *up-country* investors.

When does it hit you?

The usual stage of business at which this blunder hurts is when one is gathering critical mass in terms of liquid funds, sales turnover and profits for a take-off. Actually this is the stage at which the problem hit our friend Sharma. When the small unit is in its nascent stage, it does everything it can to get that order so necessary for sustaining itself. There is no time and resources for one to think of alternatives. The unit typically invests in assets (machines, staff, stocks) specific to the buyer in order to grow by getting more and more regular orders of this kind.

At that stage, if there are compelling economic reasons (such as recession or budget cuts), the buyer cuts back on orders and/or delays payments: most probably both. When this happens the ancillary small industry is in deep trouble. The depth of the trouble will vary by the extent of dependence and also by the mode of financing. If outside credits have been used to finance stocks and machines, insolvency stares the unit in the face; if the mode of financing is its own equity, then the game is one of much reduced turnover and forced patience. The effects of the first kind will be particularly stronger for new units which have had no time to build reserves.

Are you next in line?

The problems arising out of uncompensated asset specificity and excessive dependence on one buyer may appear in various guises. Diagnosing the extent of the danger of these problems and finding out whether you are likely to be the next victim is fairly straightforward. The entrepreneur should ask himself the questions given in Box 3.2.

BOX 3.2
How to assess if your unit will suffer from Blunder 1 and to what extent

There may be three categories of (one-way) uncompensated asset specificity and/or non-diversified market risk:

☐ The unit in question may be selling to only one PSU buyer;
☐ It is selling mostly to one private sector buyer; and
☐ It has many final users for its products but the selling arrangements rely exclusively on one intermediary.

Obviously, the combination of asset specificity and non-diversified market risk is more deadly than either one singly.

1. The units in this category are most prone to ruin due to Blunder 1. The unit may be selling to the PSU under a standing rate contract, in which case the risk is mainly due to cut-back on orders. Some level of business will continue to be forthcoming. If the focal unit is supplying by participating in tenders, then the risk is compounded as the unit will have to face competition from many others, all of whom cause the business to shrink and hence all of whom will massively undercut the prices.

2. If the sole buyer is a private sector unit, chances are good that there is a degree of co-option, if not incorporation of the focal unit in the buyer. The vendor may have been set up as a tax dodge. The owner of the buying firm may be the senior cousin or a family friend. This sort of a relationship is beset with problems of mutual squabbling and perennial whining of complaints, but the small industry unit is not really threatened. It is stunted, its financial sickness is mostly of tactical origin but it will not become insolvent.

Though the buyer and the vendor are at arm's length in reality (that is, there is no co-option or incorporation), there usually would be a written MOU or an explicit understanding between the two parties. If such an agreement exists, then the vendor's risk is caused not by whimsical behaviour on the part of the buyer, but by his commercial fortunes. The vendor needs to assess the extent and intensity of the buyer's dependence on him. If he is just one of many vendors, he will be in trouble. If he supplies a reasonable proportion of the demand of the buyer, there will be greater mutuality.

3. In this category fall those units whose ultimate buyers are many, but they have tied up with a distributor or a selling agent who is too big for them to handle. Small industries do this in order to avoid all marketing hassles. Often the distributor also finances the trade inventory. After a while, the distributor is almost invariably in a position to push the same product of a competitor, and thus your unit becomes dispensable to him, but he remains all too important to you. The distributor starts dictating terms and the same phenomenon of over-dependence repeats itself.

Obviously, the trick is to have at least two distributors, possibly in two different geographical places as soon as possible. In general, when the largest distributor is handling 40-50 per cent of your total volume, it is time to appoint one more.

This has two prerequisites. In the first place, you should not have to depend on a distributor for financing your inventory. And second, you should find time to search, short-list and appoint distributors as the sales volume increases.

For units in all categories, the important thing to consider and, if possible, change is the rigidity in fixed assets. Are the fixed assets in your unit capable of producing only your existing products or something else also? In the good old days, the village artisan could make only one kind of a traditional product: be it mud pots, shoes, carts or locks. His skill was not versatile and once market began to offer variety in the substitute products, he simply folded up. You could get hurt by a similar phenomenon at a larger scale. These are the days of dedicated facilities for very high volume, efficient production of a single product. And these machines cost the earth. Beware of buying them. If you or your family have not been marketing that or related products for a decade and hence you do not have contacts in the trade circle, stay away from such things for the first three to four years.

Basically, high asset specificity of productive assets, sole purchaser, low dependence of the buyer on the unit, high dependence on the buyer of the units are to be treated as flashing signals of danger for this blunder.

The options to avoid the blunder have been hinted at earlier. Create market diversification, versatility of fixed productive assets or at least a certain degree of mutuality of dependence.

BLUNDER 2: Biting off more than you can chew

Description of the case

Deshpande is in his late fifties. He was a very good student in his college days. He came from a well-off family but had to suddenly slog it out in his youth owing to a sudden downswing in his family's fortunes. He graduated in Economics and went on to work for some small companies manufacturing fasteners in western India.

He was a very friendly and likable man and soon became very well known among buyers of fasteners. Many a purchase manager in different companies and senior officers of many PSUs became personally known to him. He moved to Indore in the late seventies. He bought a place in the industrial area and got himself registered with the SSIDC. He set up his factory to manufacture 30 tonnes per month (TPM) of fasteners.

He had to buy the raw material from an importing PSU. Being an actual user, they used to charge him the going official prices, which were 20 per cent lower than the 'open market' prices, but he had to pay the full price in advance. The quality of the fasteners he made was generally thought to be very good and hence even the most demanding OEM company purchased his product. He sold his fasteners to OEM, most of which were private companies, as well as to the open trade where they were used for replacing the original fasteners in broken down machines.

The companies typically paid much higher prices but settled their bills after more than two months. The trade, on the other hand, paid on delivery, which meant usually a fortnight after the date of dispatch from the factory. However, the trade did not order any fasteners in five months of the year, gave massive orders in three and was so-so in the remaining four. The OEM demand was relatively more stable all through the year. Deshpande supplied to at least five companies and to over a few dozen traders. He also supplied his fasteners to some PSUs as stores items, usually when they wanted to buy on an emergency purchase basis.

On the whole, he needed working capital equal to some three months of sales for his unit, if it were to keep functioning smoothly. The general absence of demand from the traders in the rainy season added to the complications.

So successful was Deshpande in his operations that he used the factory to 55 per cent of its rated capacity for two running years. He was justifiably proud of this as the average industry performance was only 28 per cent capacity utilisation. He could also effectively use his contacts in the industry. His background in the same line proved to be very advantageous.

Deshpande had put in a million rupees at the time of starting the unit, and the loans from SSIDC amounted to another million, with the sanctioned working capital accommodation limit with the bank at another million and a half. To stretch this accommodation to almost twice as much he had to resort to adopting the 'beer crates' strategy (that is, the fairly common practice of 'befriending' important people over beer).

As a way out of his troubles, he decided to expand the capacity and invested another million and a half into an extension of his factory building and new machinery. The work was half done when recession hit. In the recession years of 1980 and 1981, payments from companies were delayed and the bank manager he dealt with was transferred. The new fellow was much less accommodative and asked him to return the money above the sanctioned limit. When he could not do so, the bank simply locked his factory. The promising and imposing castle fell like a house of cards.

What is the entrepreneur's rationale?

Deshpande even now believes that what he did was absolutely right. He argues that trade and companies *will* delay payments as long as they can. (In those days of Tandon Committee and Chore Committee norms for sanctioning working capital, small companies were used by all companies as sources of working capital to beat Tandon and Chore. Nowadays they all try to issue Commercial Paper or manipulate the markets to issue rights shares at a large premium or Zero Coupon Debentures.)

That is a part of life. One must try to sell as much as possible within the existing constraints. Hence the only sensible thing to do is to maintain good working relationships with banks. If that means having to employ 'beer crates' strategy, so be it. If not, try harder. After the bank stops helping, one must delay the payment of electricity bill to the extent possible, delay payments of sales tax—adopting legal suit and 'beer crates' strategy whenever necessary—and of course stretch every possible creditor to the limit!

For Deshpande expansion was vital if he were to make high sales in the busy season. He could not get enough money to stock the raw material or finished fasteners, so he had to get the extra capacity to manufacture more in any given month. Therefore, he put in all the generated surpluses in new building and machines. He was going to apply to the SSIDC for an enhanced loan any way; in fact he had, just six months before the fall, but we all know what

SSIDCs are. They move so slowly; it took months for them to send even an acknowledgement.

Why is this a blunder?

The blunder here is 'biting off more than you can chew'. Specifically, attempting to expand the fixed assets without providing for adequate working capital. Although many of you may disagree, this too is amazingly common across regions and sectors of the economy.

Undoubtedly, my colleagues in management will frown sternly at these rather loose terms. What do I mean by 'adequate working capital'? How is one to provide for it? If one does generate surpluses from operations like Deshpande did, should one apply them first for working capital or for expanding the fixed investment base? It would be futile to give unassailable general suggestions. Deshpande's rationale in this case was not a coherent body of interconnected logical thoughts, but intuitive assessments of situations as they kept appearing before him. And that is precisely how most entrepreneurs react: seldom taking a comprehensive view but only building up their decisions in an incremental sense.

Let me explain. In our case here, Deshpande found that his many contacts in companies and PSUs were extremely helpful in securing orders for some thing which was an inevitable industrial stores item. Like diamonds, these fasteners would be needed forever and repeatedly by the same customers, whether OEMs or traders. Apart from his contracts, he was able to make excellent fasteners and thus could get very good orders. So he naturally wanted to expand. So far so good, you might say.

Well, not exactly. The central question to ask is: what is meant by capacity? The second critical question Deshpande ought to have asked is why was the capacity utilisation in the fasteners industry as low as 28 per cent. To the first question, most people— including entrepreneurs—give a wrong answer. They would tell me in the instant case that the capacity was 30 TPM.

Certainly that was the machine capacity. Please, think through and do not make me tell you why that is *not* the pragmatic answer. The right thing to do *is* to generate internal resources, if one does not have them at the time of starting operations, for staying liquid in all normal circumstances and to acquire the strength to stay liquid in adverse times. *Unfortunately, this fundamental lesson of mercantile capitalist businesses is not appreciated or even learnt by first-generation entrepreneurs, particularly if they have a strong technical background.*

Staying liquid when business is expanding means that much more money is needed. Alternately, one must be more patient while expanding. A retired army officer who is a well-settled businessman, once told me during a casual meeting: 'You may know the best of the men in the best friendly manner. You may think the bank manager is in your pocket. But I can tell you from my experience, if you do not have your own money, then you *have to* struggle and wait before you can become big.'

Obviously, the 'beer crates' strategy fails when you get a tee-totaller bank manager. Such strategies are expensive, disreputable and myopic. They are simply not reliable enough for one to base major plans, such as expansion, on them.

What alternatives did Deshpande have?

Patience and prudence have become so old-fashioned, almost as bad as the exhortations for honesty! Are there no quick methods of getting working capital which do not prevent one from putting all one's surpluses in fixed capital? One very popular alternative is discussed in Blunder Three, and that gives you my honest opinion on how good it is.

The only possible alternatives to a blunder such as this are:

- Buying machinery on lease/hire-purchase schemes
- Using suppliers credit against hypothecation for the machinery acquired from them
- Raising money from the public in the form of unsecured deposits for working capital
- Appointing distributors or sole selling agents at a reasonably attractive premium, provided they take care of the bulk of the working capital
- Buying materials from traders who are willing to give credit, even at a high incremental cost

- Rigorously avoiding business which involves credit even if it means lower sales
- Or even, giving a stake in the firm to the buyers or the key sellers so that at least a part of the sales/purchases give relief on the working capital front.

Nothing is new about these alternatives. All such things have been tried out by different people at different times. With the near-complete opening of the banking and finance sectors, the options have really multiplied manifold. However, the need for patience and prudence, as my retired Army friend advocates, cannot be overstressed. Obviously, everything presupposes a certain set of situations and behaviours, a credibility and reputation in the market. All of them are not always possible for a small-industry unit; and none is without associated costs.

When does it hit you?

Blocking precious resources in fixed assets without taking care of the working capital requirements affects the business immediately. It first manifests itself, though most entrepreneurs do not quite realise it, in the form of reduced margins.

For a long time, fixed long-term capital had been cheaper to borrow, and instead of borrowing it, if the entrepreneur blocks his money in it then he must generate the working capital through more expensive ways and that will inevitably reduce the margins.

Traumatic ill-effects, like the one which hit Deshpande, make themselves felt only when this mistake of blocking money in fixed assets when the firm is not liquid is done recklessly or when recession in the buyer industry elongates the working capital pipeline even more than usual. At some point in time, the bank or whosoever is providing credit must call the end of the game. And if at that time the situation in the buyer industry is bad, then insolvency obviously stares the business in the face.

Are you next in line?

This becomes somewhat redundant, yet there is no denying its importance. It is redundant for an entrepreneur who is involved in his business on a day-to-day basis because he would be right on top of things.

Still, one tends to regard money as fungibles and operate the numerous bank accounts in such a manner that it is difficult to clearly identify the source and the precise use of funds. The fundamental thing to keep track of is whether one is ensuring that working capital is adequately provided for, without creating new and newer ghosts which will haunt the business at some future date. It is difficult to gauge the exact level of working capital before it is to be considered sufficient.

The questions given in Box 3.3 will help you gauge this level reasonably well, tell you whether you are taking unnecessary chances of insolvency and, finally, help you judge whether you are falling in the trap of committing Blunder 2. Some of the points on working capital are elaborated in subsequent sections as well as in the chapter on financial management.

BOX 3.3
How do you calculate the length of the pipeline and estimate the necessary working capital?

The need for working capital comes from some of the following:

- the need to make advance payment to suppliers of raw materials;
- the need to stock up raw materials in cheap season;
- the need to maintain normal stock of raw materials;
- the time period during which materials are in the production stage;
- the need to hold stock of finished goods in the factory, godown or distributors' godown; and
- the need to give trade credits.

The relevant questions to help you assess the working capital need are given below. In the chapter on financial management, a detailed example illustrates the logic and the steps for calculating working capital.

At the moment, in your existing manner of operations, do you pay for raw materials in advance of delivery? By how many days? Of course, you may be able to get the raw material on credit, in which case the working capital need is reduced.

What is the quantity of raw materials consumed and what is the amount of money needed for this length of time? How much is ordered at one time? Are there significant quantity discounts which make larger order quantities very attractive?

On an average how long does the material take to be fully processed and reach the stage of delivery for sale? (Assume the date of payment of excise as the date of delivery from the factory.)

What is the proportion of processing costs (labour charges, additional materials used and duties paid)?

Do you advance credit to your buyers? If yes, then what is the proportion of other costs such as transportation, packaging, interest, power and staff salaries to original material costs?

On an average how many days elapse between the date of delivery and the date of receipt of the payment? Are there significant differences in payment performance in different market segments? If yes, what discount would have to be given to those who pay fast? Again, your buyers may be paying for the goods in advance of the delivery. These questions will help you assess the working capital need.

In general, I would say that you have provided adequate working capital if you have kept sufficient funds to see through 10-15 per cent longer than this estimate. More importantly, if you have arranged for these funds from either your own personal funds or from specific and legitimate formal bank limits sanctioned.

How close are you to Blunder 2?

Do you keep electricity bills, telephone bills, sales tax dues, and other charges unpaid after the due date? Do you always do this? Are you forced to do this for want of money? How frequently do you have to buy stores items from or hire services of an expensive and low quality supplier simply because he gives credit? Do you or your staff ever have to cancel a business trip for want of bank balance? Do you buy even crucial stores materials only at the eleventh hour? How frequently do you have to spend hours dodging or persuading your creditors? How frequently do your cheques bounce/have to be re-presented by the payee after you do some hard work? If such things are routine, it only means that your business volume is reaching the capacity permitted by your finances.

But more importantly how often in the past have you had a credit balance outstanding with a machinery supplier/cement or steel supplier for construction, as an advance with your order when some of the above also were happening? If the answer to this question is always or even frequently, then you are very close to the blunder. If this happens occasionally, then you are developing a bad habit and only if this *never* happens then you indicate the due care.

BLUNDER 3: Borrowing in the informal money market to expand business

Description of the case

Raghavan has seen a lot of trouble in life. He worked hard in a finance sector organisation for a while and then decided to start on his own. Raghavan's family could not give him financial backing in his business. He lived in Calcutta where he dealt with traders and business associates in selling *chhanna* (a raw material used for making sweets, particularly Bengali. It is prepared by skilfully splitting warm milk) and managing his fledgling organisation.

He made good quality *chhanna* for household consumption in a factory some 500 km away. His *chhanna* was also used as an input in certain consumer goods companies of small size and stature. The raw material for making *chhanna* showed a lot of seasonality. It made sense to buy a lot of material in good season when it was going cheap, make and stock as much *chhanna* as possible and sell it in the season of scarcity some six months later. All one needed was access to storing technology, which Raghavan had.

Also, there was a great advantage in storing the manufactured chhanna for mixing with fresh *chhanna* before selling it to the buyers. Special care had to be taken for storing the *chhanna* as it was perishable. The *chhanna* was sold through a network of dealers and retailers as well as to small companies in the consumer line. There was intense generic competition in the *chhanna* line and as much of it was sold to the companies as an input, they were far more concerned with price and credit terms rather than quality per se.

The suppliers of raw material had to be given their payment within a week of delivery. The buyer companies usually took two or more months to pay their dues, whereas the dealer network paid within about two weeks of delivery. Raghavan was always tempted to make a lot of *chhanna* in the cheap season and stock it for a few months for raking in the benefit of higher prices.

Raghavan did not have many fixed assets, as the production process involved was managed using the industrial equivalent of 'a few pots and pans'. Nor did he possess any real estate worth the name. Since the *chhanna* was perishable, it was not usable as hypothecable stock. Thus, Raghavan found it very difficult to borrow money from any reputed bank. Since the need for money to finance business was always high and urgent, Raghavan had to rely on money sharks who were willing to lend as much as he wanted. Their interest rates were upwards of 3 per cent per month.

In 1994, the year in which Raghavan sold *chhanna* worth Rs 35 lakh, he also had to borrow as much as Rs 12 lakh from sundry money-lenders. Since these people were not registered money-lenders, all such transactions were informal and Dr Manmohan Singh's men neither knew anything about it nor got any share for him. In 1994, during the cheap season, Raghavan bought the raw material and stored it hoping that the prices of *chhanna* would rise in the scarce season later. Instead, they fell and Raghavan made a loss on the stocks. The sharks are now after his blood and Raghavan is perennially devising newer ways of avoiding them.

What is the entrepreneur's rationale?

Raghavan's point is simple. He feels that it is necessary and absolutely vital for any firm to do as much business as possible. This way, your product reaches more homes and hands more quickly. If you are making a good product, then so many more homes have been won over. And then your competitors have that much tougher time winning them over from you. Hence, he wished to do quantitative expansion as quickly as possible.

Also, obviously, as long as he was not selling on the basis of low price for capturing the market (and he was not such a fool as that), there was always a good margin in making *chhanna*. Therefore, the larger quantity he sold, the better off he was in terms of internal accruals for future expansion. He was temperamentally opposed to any conservatism where growth was concerned, as he felt that in today's world no customer remains unserved. His motto was: If you do not serve him someone else will.

Of course, he would have liked to use formal means of financing but there he did not seem to have any choice. He had no solid assets on which the bank could lend him money. The parental home offered no collaterals either and even if it did, why should he mix home finance and business finance? The product was perishable and that ruled out any credit against stock of the preserved *chhanna*. So what could he do? He wanted to grow in terms of business; that needed money. The bank would not give and so he took from the loan sharks, and that was that.

(Finally, he inevitably said, one had to take chances in business as—Ha!—no risk no gain!) His logic for using borrowed funds for stocking for speculative gain was: he borrowed at 3 per cent per month and hence in six months the interest amounted to 18 per cent. Since it was in cash, after tax deductions the difference was more like 36 per cent. But the difference in the prices of *chhanna* in the two seasons was 50 per cent and he still made 14 per cent in the bargain.

Why is it a blunder?

The above is a common case of a company seeking to increase its turnover in the absence of enough working capital by borrowing money in the informal cash market. This particular act or decision is probably the most prevalent among the five blunders mentioned in this chapter. It is, in fact, common enough to be considered the usual business practice.

Expansion of business (or in common business parlance *kam*

badhana, increasing the work level) is, after all, considered the only way to grow. Between the three major stages—purchase of raw material, in-process and finished goods inventories and credit against sales—at least one needs large finances for any form of business, or else the line is not worth entering at all. Thus, for industries based on seasonal agricultural produce, raw material stocks have to be maintained at some level. For fashion goods, massive stocks of the final product have to be ready in a short span and hence stocks are needed. In most industrial intermediaries, sales credit is the key to getting orders.

Cursed are those lines in which the need for large financing exists at more than one stage. In the case of Raghavan there was a need for large intermediate stocks as well as credits against sales. In all such cases, the amount of business one does is crucially defined by the amount of working capital one has. It is not surprising that most shrewd entrepreneurs keep all their own money reserved for financing working capital and use borrowed funds for fixed assets.

When one wants to do more business than the working capital permits, one ends up in a somewhat messy situation. The firm may start facing a very acute liquidity crunch: inability to pay salaries on time, difficulty in paying even excise duty to clear goods, delays in payment of all sorts of bills, perennially angry protests from suppliers, possibility of production stopping owing to absence of some critical input and so on.

To avoid all this, the firm starts borrowing in the money market where the interest rates begin at 2 per cent per month and may go as high as up to 4 per cent, depending on the desperation of the firm and its general market standing. Well. I know all this, you are saying, where does the blunder come in?

The reasons it is a blunder are twofold:

- There is a great deal of chaos introduced in operations by this kind of invited liquidity crunch. For instance, the operating people are forced to put up with goods and services given by only those people who give credit and that too at much higher than the fair prices, thus increasing the cost of business and reducing its predictability.

- There is a pressure to generate cash to pay the interest to the lenders, the usual terms being cash.

This can only be done by tying up a part of this capacity for informal business, thus reducing formal profits.

And, God forbid, if funds borrowed at such rates are used for creating speculating positions, the firm is courting bankruptcy. In fact, most of the respectable commodity traders who speculate do so on their own funds, and the more sensible industrialists stay away from speculation altogether, focusing purely on the manufacturing margins.

Let me narrate what happened to a friend of mine who invested his personal finances. He pawned his wife's gold and invested money just a few days before one of Manmohan Singh's budgets in the secondary share market, notably the high priced A group securities in BSE. The broker asked him to give only 30 per cent margin. He fell a prey to the inducement. Manmohan did not smile and the share prices went down by 15 per cent. He thus incurred a net loss of 45 per cent on his investment and lost half of his wife's gold. Borrowing money to speculate is very risky and only hardened gamblers may do it; industrialists may do it only at their peril.

What were the alternatives Raghavan had?

The alternatives which Raghavan had were simple. Either he did not speculate at all, thus avoid creating speculative stocks betting on seasonal increases in prices. If he insisted on speculative stocking, then he could have done so only if he could also tie up matching sales at future dates, thus creating a sort of understanding for delayed or deferred deliveries. This could also be done by trying to enter into agreements with one's marketing channel for obtaining credit against promise of deliveries in scarce time at predetermined rates, or the same thing with suppliers. The situation in which Raghavan found himself was naturally such that his bargaining strength in either of these options was limited. Since the loan shark was his only option, he ought to have deferred the decision to do speculative borrowings till the firm had its own accruals.

When does it hit you?

Between the desire to do larger volume of business with existing fixed assets and the ability to do so with the available working capital, there is always a gap. And this gap perhaps persists right through to the very top of the industrial pyramid. Only when the company has extremely well established brands and/or operates in monopolistic markets, does it operate with *negative* working capital, that is, having excess current liabilities than current assets.

Witness, for example, how Bajaj or Maruti Udyog used to have mammoth unsecured outside funds in the form of deposits for booking vehicles. In the consumer goods sector, Ponds, Johnson and Johnson and Levers enjoy stiff terms like cash-before-delivery so that their working capital requirement is nearly zero. Such companies have to worry about making prudent use of their liquid funds. Trade practices in some primary goods allow low working capital business. Thus, in the oil seeds line, one can buy on 11-day credit, and if one is able to sell in cash, working capital will not be a problem. Again, small industries engaged in speciality products such as special machinery can manage with low levels of working capital.

But for most of the other companies and certainly a majority of small industries, perceived business opportunities will continue to exceed the level permitted by available finance for working capital. So, this problem and the possibility of this blunder seriously jeopardising the business keep haunting the entrepreneur at almost every stage.

The business units which try to use credit as a weapon to achieve greater sales are definitely courting trouble. The trouble with these decisions comes the moment there is some degree of sluggishness in demand or recessionary trend in the buyer industry. In 1993, average payment periods experienced by the steel industry in the throes of recession were over six months! Imagine your plight if you were one of *their* suppliers and had borrowed in the cash market for supplying to them. The trouble also keeps occurring in commodity markets which have highly fluctuating prices. In fact, most prudent businesses are now trying to shift in favour of cash-on- if not before-delivery.

Are you next in line?

Actually, as this as well as the previous blunder have to do with working capital aspects, the set of diagnostic questions is bound to be shared. If one ignores the last para from Box 3.3 (which is about the supreme folly of investing in fixed assets without enough working capital), then the rest of the questions are relevant.

I will supplement these with some more to cover borrowing in the cash markets and borrowings for financing speculative stocks. See Box 3.4 for that purpose.

BOX 3.4
Assessing closeness to Blunder 3

Box 3.4 helps you to identify the working capital need. The following questions are in addition to those given in Box 3.3 and are focused on informal borrowings.

1. Have you borrowed funds from friends and relatives as short-term unsecured deposits? Have you exhausted the possibilities of such borrowings? Do you pay interest on these deposits in cash or cheque? How do you account for the cash spent for interest payments? How do you generate it? Do you pay cash interest because they demand it or because you wish it to be cash?

There really is no reason to pay cash interest to your friends and relations. It reduces your formal turnover and profits, for their benefit. They may have money of different colours and want good returns on it. That is their problem, not yours. Offer them two to three per cent more than the best bank rate and no more. But most entrepreneurs want to pay cash as they themselves are doing a tax fiddle!

2. How frequently do you borrow from the informal money market (moneylenders and traders) against *hundies*? How frequently do you keep extending these *hundies*? These are the real troublemakers. They are quite used to the techniques of recovery and also have extensive trade contacts. Any significant reliance on them is bad for your long-term growth, peace of mind or social status.

3. How frequently do you buy materials well over your usual monthly/quarterly requirement merely because they are going cheap? How frequently do you boast about what a smart businessman you are as you made such a lot of money on stock profits? Do you really believe that you are in for making stock profits, or you feel that you must look at manufacturing margins? If you believe making stock profits is so clever and crucial, shouldn't you really restrict yourself to trading alone?

4. Have you borrowed cash to do some of your 'smart' buying of seasonally available material? Have you got bills for that stock? Is that stock insured? Is it shown in your stock register? In case of stock loss due to adverse prices or material deterioration, can you charge it to your profit and loss account?

Some times what happens is that because the source of financing is informal (i.e., black), the whole chain of transactions is in black. That way you block your production capacity for black transactions. You remain small on books!

Options to avoid and their costs

There are two issues involved here. The first is whether and how you should buy large stocks of seasonally available materials. The second is how to manage your working capital requirement without getting into cash borrowings. As far as the issue of buying huge stock of materials in season is concerned, my suggestion is that you should simply not do so on borrowed funds. Gamble if you must, but gamble only when you have enough money to pay for the loss which can accrue. I personally would strongly recommend completely refraining from speculative or seasonal stocking in the absence of adequate staying power, whether these finances are actually deployed in the business or not.

Even non-speculative business moves can entail cash borrowings. There are three options for avoiding getting stuck in this mistake and the morass it creates. The soundest is, of course, to keep the volume of business well within the limits permitted by available formal, white finances. This conservative policy gives a great deal of strength and solidity to the firm. When the market knows that your firm will pay its obligations on or a day before it is due, the market starts falling over itself to serve your firm, offers you premium-quality goods and services, quotes very reasonable prices and even gives you discounts on them. Over the years, the general image of the firm becomes very formidable and that itself is a highly valuable asset in getting prestigious contracts and orders. Such a firm can also take real advantage of its high overall liquidity in providing credit in that rare event which gets it very advantageous orders. Of course, it takes time to build such a reputation and image.

The second option is to enter into dialogues and agreements with two or three parties and appoint them as sole selling distributors in their respective territories provided they make spot payment irrespective of the time at which payment is made by the final buyer. This procedure is often adopted by many an industry, particularly in the industrial raw materials sector. This way you eliminate the need to finance trade credits and inventories. There is always the risk of committing Blunder 1 in this option. But if you have two to three such dealers then you do not become over-dependent on any one.

The third is to try and enter into job-work contracts with buyers by persuading them to invest in speculative buying. In the oil trade, there are occasions when large marketers like ITC or Marico might want to do the buying of seeds, stock it and get it processed in the jobber's premises. If you are the jobber, then your capacity utilisation objective is met and you also make your manufacturing margin, without the risk.

BLUNDER 4: Weaving a web of commercial deception

(There is just one caveat to what follows: I have no desire to moralise regarding old-fashioned virtues of probity and honesty. I write the following only from the limited perspective of its implications for growth.)

Description of the case

Shakeel was schooled in Delhi and thereafter did his vocational training in an ITI. He was good at his work and became a turner. After some years of working with a company, he decided to set up on his own.

He got some informal loan from a steel trader and bought a general-purpose lathe machine. He started doing some finishing operations on components made by his neighbour and cousin and was paid on a piece-rate basis. He was found to do a good job, and the company which bought from his cousin came to him for doing the job directly. Gradually, Shakeel started doing more and more operations for the company on a piece-rate basis till he discovered that a particular component had a lot of demand.

He started making this component, which was used as an item for industrial applications by several small companies. He first started doing the entire set of operations himself but soon discovered the good old virtues of division of labour. He also found out that if he took money from the loan shark, promising to pay 3 per cent per month, and then bought raw material, doing some operations himself and the rest on piece-rate basis from smaller job workers, he could make a lot of money.

He applied himself in this line. He started doing business worth some Rs 18 lakh per month, of which at least 9 lakh was spent on steel, another 1 lakh on payment to the job workers and some Rs 50,000 on interest. He still made a lot of money and, wonderfully, all of it was completely without encumbrances of tax and accounting.

All his job workers did work in cash, the loan was in cash, the raw material was obtained in cash and there was virtually no record of any kind. He kept a few illegible notes in a dirty copybook in the top shelf of his 'loaded' cupboard. All went well. He changed his scooter every month and his car every Diwali. His wife became a cause for jealousy among other women as she bought a gold necklace every alternate month. The component was in demand, the loan shark happy with his repayment record, the little job workers happy for all the work he gave them and Shakeel himself thought all was for the best in the best of all possible worlds.

Then one day the buyer of a bigger company came and asked

him for a bill. Well, he wrote on a piece of paper on his notebook, stamped it with his Shakeel Enterprises stamp and gave it to the buyer. An unexpected trouble arose. The buyer came the next day with a smart guy in a shining Maruti 1000, who took one look at Shakeel and made a face.

He somehow managed to straighten his face and started talking about orders which were far beyond Shakeel's wildest dreams. The smart guy also told him that the workmanship of Shakeel and gang was very good and it was a pity they could not be given this truly massive opportunity because he would have to convince the foreign collaborator that this component could be made in India. The collaborator had seen the pieces and had approved, but before he agreed for standardising on buying from Shakeel, he wanted to have a look at Shakeel's operations, plant, material handling system, quality control procedures, etc. He was to come after six months and had asked the smart guy to sort out these matters and find out what kind of a deal would Shakeel want for 'sourcing' the component on a regular basis. Price, it seemed, was less important than having the proper procedures for getting the ISO 9002 mark. But could Shakeel show any thing in six months?

With orders like that in reach, Shakeel was sure that it was possible, as he had a lot of money, jewellery and so on to get a good project going. He approached a management consultant (not me, someone else!) who made an impressive report for Shakeel. Though Shakeel could hardly understand it, he took the report (which indicated what a sound project it was though it needed Rs 3 crore in fixed investment) and the consultant to an investment banker, a venture capital funder and an SSIDC all in the span of a week.

They all got back to him and said that the project looked viable and wonderful but they wanted documents: balance sheets, P and L accounts, bank account details and so on. Shakeel took his balance sheet showing massive assets amounting to Rs 1,35,000 and a P and L account showing a sales figure of Rs 11 lakh in the previous accounting year.

The term-lending institution was the most polite of the lot and told Shakeel to forget about the project. The investment banker told him to have a glass of water and go away, muttering *pata nahin kahan kahan se chale aate hain!* ('God knows where they turn up from!') under his breath.

It appears that all that jewellery and all that cash were just no substitute for properly audited accounts of sizeable figures if his project, involving investments of Rs 3 crore was to be taken seriously. When the foreign collaborator showed up in six months, he fixed a deal with Shakeel's rival who always used to rave and rant about the IT department taking away all his money, but paid it to them all the same.

Shakeel was wondering what hit him. When the consultant met him again, he told the consultant: *'Are bhai, ye sab bekar hai. Hame aur kam badhana hi nahin hain. Kya karna hai ye sab karake?'* ('Oh, well, all this trouble is pointless. I really do not want to expand. Why should I?')

What was the entrepreneur's rationale?

In the above case, I can vouch for the fact that Shakeel did not do the business informally *because* he wanted to evade taxes. He was actually paying more money to the tax consultant who bribed the sales tax and income tax people than he would have to pay as tax. The point is that he felt that doing business formally is 'too much headache'.

And it must be honestly stated in favour of Shakeel that he had really not thought that he could grow all that big as to make a smart white man feel that their company can source components from him. His self-perception was very modest. Though he was making a lot of money, he was really and truly respectful towards all that was 'educated and refined'.

At the moment all he had to do was to keep very minimal records about the pieces of component to be supplied, the number of pieces given to smaller job-workers at any given time and the moneys due to be paid to them. If he were to do the business formally then he would have to maintain all sorts of inward and outward stock registers, keep transit insurances, bills of lading, invoices, credit and debit notes, bank statements and so on.

Given his background and education, working habits, language used and so on, it was difficult for him to get some one to do it properly for him and maintain a proper business record. Nor did he have the time or the patience to do such things himself. So the better and definitely far simpler thing was to hire this tax consultant and pay him through the nose for keeping the tax men happy. And the seemingly irrefutable logic was topped by a very sad but true statement *'Yeh sab kagaj rakhane ke bad bhi to unhe khilana hi padata hai. Phir kyon ham jhanjhat men pade?'* ('Even after maintaining all these records, I have to bribe all these fellows. Then why should I take all this trouble?')

Why is it a blunder?

Let us be honest: this sort of attitude is a typical cause of 'voluntary sickness' in a firm. The productive capacities of the firm are used for transacting decent volumes of business. However, as much as possible, if not most of the business, is done informally to avoid paying income tax, sales tax, excise duties and so on. In fact, a lot of businessmen think that doing business in such a manner is the ultimate in smart behaviour.

Three things are in favour of such logic. In the first place, for a long time in the past and to a total novice like me even now, the formalities of tax documentation and records are very complex. One often feels that they are nothing short of a deliberate conspiracy between tax departments and tax consultants. To be honest and truthful is also very troublesome; that is a stark reality.

Second, it is a great pity but it is true that even the honest tax-payer has to bribe the very tax department people if he is to avoid harassment. I am not about to make futile statements about fall in moral standards in public services, deteriorating national character, etc. but it does happen to be the truth in many cases. A humorous anecdote is a nice way of illustrating this point.

A friend of mine once told me that when he took his monthly returns to the local Central Excise office for filing, he found a regular monthly cash *hafta* had to be contained in the envelope. Once, he forgot to put it. The clerk opened the envelope, saw the returns, searched some more in the envelope and finding nothing there said, *'Bhai, mujhe to kuch nazar nahin aa rahan hai. Jao bade sahab se baat karake sare kagaz le aao.'* ('Brother, I cannot see anything here, so go and talk to your senior and come back with all the papers.') The moment the usual *hafta* was put in the envelope, normal vision returned to the clerk. He could see the records!

Finally, there are so many palms to be greased even in the so-called liberalised industrial environment. So rampant is the practice that not greasing the palms is deliberately inviting delays and trouble. Nor is this statement particularly bold or incredible. So many researches into the extent of bribery and palm greasing in different departments in different states, industries, departments, and so on, have been published that one can practically write a review paper on the subject.

And I know of no officer who is willing to take his bribe by way of a demand draft or cheque, so cash has to be generated. Large companies manage such things through the entertainment account but even there they have to generate *cash* some how. Devoid of bright professional accounting help, poor small entrepreneurs have to simply do business without issuing bills. Most small entrepreneurs will tell you that this is the main reason why they do cash business.

I wish this were the case. My own guess is that for managing all sorts of bribes in the normal circumstances, no more than ten per cent of the business will have to be transacted in cash. In some exceptional industries such as potable liquor and some sections of the pharmaceutical industry, this may rise somewhat. I will grant even twenty per cent business in cash, thus partly making up the cash need for paying interest to friends as well as to sharks.

However, doing ninety per cent of sales without bills is not good in any circumstance. And the Shakeel who tells me that mere documentation hassles are making him do the whole business in black is expecting sympathy from the wrong quarters. There are things like open gutters, plague, tax laws and tax men in this world and one must live in the world despite them. And live one must so as not to forego all the decent and big opportunities.

Asking or allowing your tax consultant to manipulate your account (in Delhi the chap asks you, *'aapaka sale kha jaun?'* ('Shall I simply gobble up your sale,' meaning hide it utterly and completely) is falling victim to a myopic and cheap gimmick. You invite far more trouble than you avoid.

The fundamental fact is that if your firm is to grow at the least cost then you must use institutional finances. These are available only if your audited, documented accounts look respectable. You cannot ask for a loan of a crore when you have only a thousand with you. An investment banker who tells my Shakeel to go drink a glass of water and go away when he asks for a loan of three crores on the strength of accounts showing assets worth a lakh-and-a-half is being more polite than warranted. What would his boss say if he were to recommend the case? Or imagine what would SEBI have to say to the eventual public issue. Or think what those nosy new issue analysts would have written!

Any act which detracts from making your accounts look solid and good is a myopic act. If you intend to grow to become an industrial giant then you must try and bring as much of your transactions on books as possible. You may, through intelligent accounting practices, avoid tax and minimise tax liability but never, never, evade taxes by reducing your formal sales and profits.

An excellent chartered accountant from Nagpur once told me that he measures his performance in a client's case by two parameters:

- By the percentage by which he has increased the net profit figure on the books; and
- By the magnitude by which he has managed to reduce the tax burden on him simultaneously (compared to the estimates given by the client.)

The profession offers a diversity of opinions, views and advice on the subject. However, common sense dictates that doing business in cash, i.e., without allowing it to be reflected in the account books, is a myopic and counter-productive policy for firms on the path of growth.

What were the alternatives Shakeel had?

The question is this: Assuming that our Shakeel did not want to be dishonest in tax matters, but wanted to minimise his tax liabilities without jeopardising progressive consolidation and growth in things like net worth and reserves, what options did he have?

Alternately, how does he go about arranging his business so that his fear of documentation does not cripple him. Mind you, the two questions are different and need different answers. The answers to these questions are likely to raise controversy about business ethics and I surely do not wish to pontificate. Suffice it to say that under any circumstances, he would have to pay some taxes if he were to show profits. It is impossible to pay zero taxes and yet continue accumulating assets and increasing net profits year after year. Only a few people, such as the greatest industrial fast operators of the country, can perform such miracles.

When does it hit you?

This business of informal dealings invariably hurts when one is trying to shake off a shady image and stake a claim to one's place in the sun. And this happens because small figures in the past annual accounts look very bad in the sunlight.

The second occasion it may hurt is very obvious: no matter what the tax consultants tell you, there is simply no bribe in the world which will utterly, completely and irrevocably destroy all the evidence of the income actually having been earned. There are far too many linkages an average industrial undertaking has with the outside world for this to happen.

What usually happens is that the ill-gotten gains make a particular incumbent officer look the other way. But then officers change, they get transferred, your equations in the market change, priorities of the business partners, associates, buyers and sellers also change. And the tax matters can be reopened for such a long time.

As Shakespeare rightly said, 'Oh! what a complex web we weave when we first practice to deceive.' And like a spider, too many industrialists manage to get caught in this complex web of deception of their own creation.

Are you next in line?

As I candidly admitted, there is always and for all businesses a need to do some underhand dealings in cash, or taking some liberties with one's accounts for taking care of bribes and speed moneys. The question is when is it being done just for that and when for satisfying the greed of the entrepreneur himself?

Please ask yourself:

- Are your assistants doing the operating part of informal business as a matter of routine or do they invariably do the business formally but need your specific instruction for taking liberties?

[Also ask yourself]

- How much money is actually spent in payment of cash bribes and gratifications and how much by way of interest on cash borrowings? Find out whether the amount of business transacted in cash just matches this or far exceeds it.

In analysing this dishonesty be honest with yourself. If the cash income generated is far more than the need, take heed. You are basically hurting your own long-term interests.

BLUNDER 5: Becoming anonymous by multiplying

Description of the case

Kunal Shah is the eldest son. His father came to Kagaznagar 40 years ago and was among the first chemical engineers in the country. As Kagaznagar was located close to the jungle which supplied raw material for a paper mill, it had several advantages. Labour was plentiful and cheap, land was going abegging, the paper mill needed some one to supply acid who could be trusted for quick deliveries and so on. The Shah family began to make acid for almost exclusive consumption of the paper mill. The raw materials needed for its manufacture were imported and much energy was wasted in obtaining licences, quota and actual allotment from the Nigam for the raw materials.

The firm made only acid for some 20 years but then it started making super acid, unhydrous acid crystals and ferro-acidate, three related products which could be made from either the same raw materials, or from acid itself or from the by-products of acid manufacture. The combined sale of the four products soon crossed Rs 1 crore a year.

The firm would have come under the purview of the Excise Rules, but for the clever moves of Kunal Shah Senior, on the advice of Chalu and Company, their advisers in tax and accounts matters. What they did was to register three firms. One was called Kunal Shah Isolates. The second was called Jagandamaba Unhydrous. The third was called Kunal Shah and Sons and the original firm was called Kagaznagar Acids (P) Ltd. All the firms operated from the same office with the same staff working for them. Some staff were shown as employees of one firm and some of another, but work was done commonly. Their 'factories' too were in the same compound.

The firms had separate power connections, SSI registration, Sales Tax numbers and so on. The labour records were arranged in such a manner that while none of them suffered loss of pay, the liabilities under various laws were minimised. The telephone bills, petrol and car maintenance, entertainment and such other overheads were finally debited to that account which showed some profits despite the best efforts of Chalu and Company's accounting acrobatics. The tax liability was thus reduced. Also, the overall tax liability of members of the Kunal Shah family had also to be looked into.

The firms borrowed funds from the SSIDC and entered into arrangements with the bank for working capital. There were the usual issues of managing the equations. Kunal Shah ensured that there was the right amount of 'sickness' in the firms so that they could take advantage of the modified repayment schedules, conversions of debt and so on, common when near-default situations arise. And there were also the court cases.

Then, in the nineties two things happened. Senior Kunal Shah went to demolish the Babri mosque by joining the appropriate party, leaving minor things like proper management of the business to his eldest son. The son, our friend Kunal Shah, wanted to become a big industrialist and was sick of being just the *Bade*

Bhaisahab for his *munims* who only took orders from *Babuji*, i.e., Kunal Shah Senior.

Second, the government also misbehaved. It not only introduced MODVAT, it also more or less finished the regime of limits within which production could occur without having to pay excise duties. The company, patron of our Kunal Shah for ages, no longer needed this supplier as it could simply claim back the excise duty paid under the MODVAT procedures and hence could afford to buy from big suppliers. So it stopped buying. Also, Kunal Shah Senior had maintained a cordiality of relations with other buyers which could not be continued and in the absence of any tax advantage, they too started showing wavering signs.

In these circumstances, Kunal Shah wondered how to handle things so that a single, reputed firm could be created out of all these 'firmlets'. That seemed absolutely necessary as now onwards acid and its derivatives could be sold only according to quality. Such quality was possible only by a thorough modernisation of the factories belonging to the four firms and that needed an investment of a few crores. Besides, there were new opportunities which he wished to tap. But what worried him was that none of the four firms seemed a respectable enough parent for the large firm to be floated as a public limited company.

What was the entrepreneur's rationale?

Kunal Shah was himself not fully in a position to give me the rationale for splitting the firms as his father had taken the decision. The decision to float a plethora of firms was taken in the early seventies. At that time, I understand, there were different limits on size of the firm up to which excise duties were not payable, interest rates were different, labour laws could be avoided and so on. The incidence of excise duties does two things: compels the need to arrange for a whole set of documentation and the inevitable increase in the price at which the product can be sold.·

Since it was one of those intermediate products the quality of which was a matter of indifference, and as other small units could deliver acid of comparable quality, it was purchased on price consideration alone. At least so Kunal Shah Senior perceived. So it was absolutely essential to avoid paying excise duties. Later, it seemed as if the pricing of the acid given to the sister firm offered a great scope for managing profit and loss accounts of both the firms. Accounting flexibility was thought to be important. So they continued to split the firms.

Why is it a blunder?

Again, I must emphasise that this is a blunder only from the point of view of the *growth* of the industry. The very need for division is artificial and leads to all sorts of complications. And all this merely for saving minor amounts on taxes or worse still, for depriving the labour force of their rightful dues in facilities under the law. The latter is essentially a sign of pettiness, and can never contribute to maintaining sustainable friendly relations with labour.

The former makes sense only if the firm is unable to fight out the battle in the market on the quality front. For that very reason this *becomes* a blunder even if it is not one to begin with: this proliferation of firms and their insignificant individual size makes these firms and their products completely faceless and anonymous. The entrepreneur just does not feel like exploring development of competitive advantages based on product quality, features or mastery of technical applications thereof.

The absence of excise levy gives it an advantage of some 10-15 per cent in price, and that is used to get orders. This may often be taken by showing prices comparable to those firms who pay excise duties, do a bit of over-invoicing and sharing the cut with the buyer. (This practice of getting a 'cut' is rampant in a large number of units. The 'cut and over-invoicing' technique is so well known that there are industry standards for it! Even investment bankers agree that as long as the extent of over-invoicing is just 10 per cent, it is fine.)

Going by this route of achieving anonymity through multiplication, the entrepreneur is firmly caught in the low-level equilibrium trap of dubious dealings for selling shoddy stuff and making a bit of black money. If I offend some of my readers by my language, I must confess my preference in calling a spade a spade. The above route certainly does not spell the makings of a giant. So well known is this practice of spawning 'paper firms' for avoidance of tax that the tax man demands his cut and that means more cash has to be generated. Hence Blunder 4. Also as each one of these 'firmlets' is strangled by tax-avoidance-oriented accounting, rarely if ever, do they have good financial credibility and hence low access to working capital. So there is a need to borrow in the informal market and so Blunder 3 gets committed and so on.

The message is clear: even if you must spawn fictitious firms for tax purposes, ensure that at least one of them is large enough and is allowed to become large.

What were Kunal Shah's alternatives?

Kunal Shah had two alternatives. The zero-option, the way I would prefer, is not to engage in this pettifogging at all. The mere saving of excise duty should not be your competitive advantage. To gain that vital cutting edge you must develop product features as well as reputation for reliability, punctuality and quality.

The second option is to increase the number of firms but keep one as a strong core firm. That core should be promoted, advertised, used for all important purposes and so on. Financially it should be sound, and there should be no accounting acrobatics about it. The rest of the units are for your accounting creativity and for other purposes. So when you want to step out of the shadows, you have at least one solid company to show to prospective investors.

When does it hit you?

Achieving anonymity through multiplication hurts you for two reasons. First, you remain anonymous, except to your immediate circle of friends, suppliers and buyers. There is no public image. Second, the gimmick hurts you because you have a dozen firms all of them too small in net worth for any banker to take you seriously. Both these hurt you when you are about to embark upon the path of growth.

4

And the Three Lesser Blunders

BLUNDER 6: Marketing myopia

Description of the cases

I shall give a series of examples for this blunder.

1. Khan makes wires which are used for winding transformers and motors. There are some five parameters (length, thickness at several points, strength in terms of ability to carry weight, toughness in terms of resisting abrasion and the ability to be tightly wound) on which the quality of a lot of wires can be measured.

For a given lot of wire to be certified as being of high quality, there are elaborate testing procedures laid down for verifying whether the ISI standards on these parameters are met. Elaborate facilities for testing are necessary. To produce wires which meet the norms on all the five parameters, a lot of care is needed at the various manufacturing stages. Supervision has to be tight, intermediate samples have to be taken, whole lots may have to be reprocessed and so on.

Buyers from reputed companies are always coming to Khan to persuade him to start sending material to them if it meets the standards. They want to develop more sources of wires for their companies. Traders from Delhi and other north Indian cities buy winding wires and in turn give them to rewinders. They generally do not fuss over details.

Khan has actually installed all the facilities for the testing. Even after he spots the deficiencies in a particular lot of wires, he prefers to sell it to the traders from Delhi rather than reprocess it. He is willing to get a few rupees less for his wires. His argument is: 'Who will take all this hassle of reprocessing? The traders from Delhi take it; may be they are not as well known as the companies which these buyers represent. But am I here to win awards or to earn money? I think I ought to sell what I make to whoever buys it and make or allow as little fuss as possible. Let the final buyer beware!'

2. Vishwakarma is engaged in producing some stuff for the food industry. He sells it both to small-time hoteliers as well as household consumers. The latter material goes under his brand name (*Vishwakarma Super*). While making his product, he has to ensure that a good quality preservative is added to the raw material. With good quality preservative, its shelf-life is three months and without it, just under a month.

Hoteliers who use the stuff are quite willing to accept a slightly inferior stuff, as it goes as an ingredient of cooked food. They appear to believe that some cunning combination of Indian curry powders can hide the quality of stuff. But housewives tend to be very finicky about the quality. They start raising Cain at the very first sign of dropping standards in terms of taste, flavour, form, shape or colour.

Despite the fact that hoteliers pay per unit a price some 20 per cent less than household consumers and pay that after two to three months, Vishwakarma sells some 60 per cent of his production to hoteliers. Absence of sales network, or a question of high volumes or problem of capacity do not make him do so. As usual, to get high quality production, supervision, care and processing have to be just right and that is a big hassle. He feels that he cannot lean on his staff and systems so hard continuously as to make stuff of the high quality which household consumers expect.

3. The story of the third entrepreneur, Panchal, is even more hard hitting. He makes metallic sheets. They are used by auto ancillaries for making components sold to big-time auto giants in India. Strictly speaking, Panchal is a medium-scale and not a

small-scale industry. But for the sake of explaining this peculiar decision-making, scale does not really matter.

The metallic flats are made after playing around with the base metal in a variety of ways: alternately heating and cooling, hammering, rolling, stretching, etc. The sequence and specific method of such playing around actually determine how good the flats are going to be for making the components.

At times, his buyers come screaming to Panchal that the flats he has sent them are no good. What then happens is somewhat as follows:

(i) If the general price of flats has somehow dipped after the sales, Panchal accuses them of wanting to return the flats merely because they can be obtained cheaper. In other words he flatly refuses the existence of any problem with his flats.

(ii) If the buyer is generally a good fellow and has been paying in time, this line is not adopted. What is done is that Panchal's sales fellow keeps telling the buyer how only he has been complaining that the flats sent are bad while all the others are happy with the lot. Any attempts by the buyer to find out who the other sufferers are and whether they got the same lot of flats are generally rebuffed.

(iii) If this line is also not helpful, and the buyer is screaming too loudly, Panchal agrees to take a sample of the flats back, either does testing on it or just pretends having done so. After this, he sends his brother, an ace metallurgist to bombard the buyer with his technical knowledge. The brother goes and does his job with aplomb and comes back triumphant.

At times the brother even ridicules the customers in his eagerness to drive home the point. The customers, cowed down, or at least seeming to be cowed down by this metallurgist, quietly scrap the flats and start searching for an alternate supplier.

4. The fourth story is quite moving. It certainly made the importer move to another supplier. Mishra had earned a good reputation for making carpets. So the importer from a cash-rich country came and talked with Mishra. He found that the carpets were good. But he wanted some change in the dimensions and

also in the patterns to be woven on the carpets. He was not even talking about prices. But there came the snag. Mishra was offended when he was told to change the dimensions and patterns. He said to the sales agent who was doing the rounds with the importer: 'Look, we have been making these carpets for two generations now. The patterns and the sizes are completely standardised. In fact, they are so clearly identified with my Mishra Kaleen Udyog that any time you see carpets of this type you can be sure it is made by us. I am not going to make any other kind of carpets just for this guy. If he wants, he can import this type or else he can make alternate arrangements.' The importer made alternate arrangements.

What was the entrepreneurs' rationale?

What I have been discussing so far are different manifestations of marketing myopia, an apt term coined by Theodore Levitt, a Harvard marketing guru. Levitt's message in the article titled thus was that firms should think of themselves as providing a certain service, which could be done by their product or by any other existing or future product. They should be committed to providing that service and not producing that product. I use the term marketing myopia in its even more earthy, immediate sense. That way I also include marketing astigmatism in it.

The entrepreneur suffering from marketing myopia insists on selling what he has or makes rather than making what the customers want. He gets wrapped up in the products which he makes and the way he makes them. Why do they do so? Since I have given various manifestations of this rather common mistake, I offer different explanations of the phenomenon. Let me start with the metallurgist Panchal.

What he tends to do is to either accuse the buyer of using quality of the flats as a pretext to return the material and get cheaper one from alternative sources, or accuse him of being unnecessarily finicky or even incompetent. The undertone, explained to me while rationalising this behaviour, is that I am right, the customer is either a rogue or an idiot. Many customers, it is true, are fair-weather friends and try to use the slightest pretext for driving a harder price bargain. Almost all the customers know less metallurgy than Panchal's brother. What is problematic is not Panchal's perception that the customers are either rogues or idiots but his way of saying so. And even more problematic is the completely unshakeable complacence about the quality of one's own stuff.

In the case of the food products Vishwakarma, the rationalisation was truly staggering. He argued that to produce food stuff of the quality housewives wanted, he had to buy high quality (with a purity level of 98 per cent or higher) preservatives, stabilising agents, flavours, emulsifiers, etc., and they were, naturally, so much more expensive. Also, their suppliers insisted on spot payment. On the other hand, the chap from whom he bought these items gave him credit for three months. As he was always short on working capital, he had to buy these items only at 75 per cent purity level.

The extent of deterioration to which Blunders 2 or 3 can take your firm, is, I hope, crystal clear. Vishwakarma would have liked to buy high quality ingredients and make high quality foodstuff but is prevented by poor financial management practice from doing so. So he is compelled to take the stance that he will sell what he makes and not make what is needed.

In the case of Khan involved in making winding wires, it is marketing myopia induced by opportunism. His wires were, in fact, bought by these lesser known (and not worth knowing) traders. They in turn gave them to fly-by-night manufacturers who are generally said to infest Delhi and other north Indian cities.

(It is, I am told, quite educating to try buying some scooter components from the spares shop. The shop owner offers you a 'standard' item, by which he means that it is made by a reputable firm. That is usually quite expensive. Then he takes out another piece and says this is from Delhi. That turns out to be at half the price. And you have Delhi items for every auto spare you can think of. According to the trade grapevine, whether these products work for five years or three seconds is entirely dependent on the buyer's horoscope.)

Khan did this kind of selling because it gave him ready sales, caused no fuss, and he was any way safe in anonymity. It also avoided reprocessing, which would have used up some capacity.

His argument, unbeatable it seems, is that he is not in business to win awards but is there to make money.

Unfortunately, a man is known by the company he keeps and a business man by the regular customers he has. By selling mainly to fly-by-night traders, Khan is also making a statement regarding himself. He is declaring himself as the shady maker of unreliable goods. Whether such an identity is what you wish to have for your business is for you to decide. I know for certain that this is no way to grow.

The last case is very difficult to classify as marketing myopia. The opinions within the Mishra family irrespective, in a way it is also true that the charm of the ethnic products tends to be lost if one were to unthinkingly monkey around with the traditional patterns. The Mishra in question brought in issues like traditional family values and cultural identity. The same is true in much stronger measure of several ethnic products and cultural artifacts which command a huge market if only some changes are made in them to suit the market.

The question in another context may be put thus: Exponents of Hindustani classical music often live in penury and have to be supported by the state. On the other hand, utter trash, played loudly and shamelessly over many a public transport music system and tea shop adding to the cacophony of noise pollution has such a large market that the kids who yell out these so-called songs become millionaires overnight.

Are the exponents of classical music myopic? Is Bhimsen Joshi wrong in not jumping like a monkey screaming dubious *double entendre*? Undoubtedly no. But then he should not mind doing so if he were seeking 'commercial growth' of his 'vocal music business' (God, how awful this combination of words sounds!).

The issue in this case is whether there is an adequate basis for the entrepreneur to regard the traditional size, shape and patterns important enough to disregard new business opportunities. To the extent this attachment to traditions is based on genuine cultural beliefs and values, there can be no quarrel with the position of Mishra, but to the extent it could just be pigheadedness on his part, it needs to be changed. While the Bhimsen Joshis of the world are absolutely right in refusing to allow cheap commercialism pollute their art, not all singers are Bhimsen Joshis and most want to be commercially successful.

Why is it a blunder?

The reason any myopia is a blunder is quite simple to state: it is short-sighted behaviour and ignores opportunities and realities. The fact is that the market does not change and adapt to the producer; it is the producer who has to do the adaptive act, at least when he is a small and weak player who has no means of making the market demand what he has to offer.

By and large, it is seldom that a marketer is able to *make* the market demand what he has to offer. His monopoly position may make the market accept him with resignation. His repetitive ad campaigns may shift the demand in his favour; but very rarely to the exclusion of other products when a choice actually is available, and even more rarely for all times to come.

Much has been written about marketing myopia and it needs hardly any elaboration. The obstinate and myopic statement of Henry Ford ('We will make any car model as long as it is Model T and we shall paint it any colour as long as it is black!') and the fall of Ford Motors from its premier position is sufficient to drive home the point.

When does it hit you?

This blunder affects the enterprise when the entrepreneur loses the pulse and the feel of the market and becomes complacent about his products. It also affects the enterprise when the entrepreneur starts becoming too preoccupied with short-term and convenient gains ignoring long-term relationships with the clients. There are many ways in which myopia sets in. Some of these are explained below.

(i) In the first way, for whatever reasons (the advantage of being the first domestic producer, sound technical knowledge, excellent contacts with major buyers, etc.), the entrepreneur is in a position to grab a decent market share and is able to use a large part of his capacity. That sets in complacence. The firm makes no efforts to keep track of the changes in consumer behaviour, factors which are influencing the demand, technological changes that may be occurring, the doings of the direct and potential competitors, etc. At first the complacence is not very dysfunctional as the buyers continue to rely on the firm for historical reasons. Then slowly the competitors make inroads in the market, the demand profile changes or the requirements of the buyers change. The firm is caught in the sands of soporific complacence and wakes up too late to find that most of the market has evaporated from under its very nose. This sort of a thing is more likely to happen for entrepreneurs who have also been committing Blunder 1.

(ii) In the second way, the entrepreneur is firmly in the mind-set of the shortage economy. Such a thing is likely to happen only if he actually enjoyed near-monopoly status sometime in the past. He then starts believing that buyers have no choice at all. 'Where will they go?' is the usual logic.

The newspaper vendor of the housing colony I once lived in had this belief. When people complained to him about missing deliveries, delays or other aspects of poor service, he often dared to reply: 'See, this is the way it will be, do you want me to continue to give you your newspaper?' The colony was poorly located and he had scared the competitors off. Many of us thought we did not have a choice, till finally one day some young people got together and started buying their papers every day during the course of a long morning walk. Unless the product or service is essential, people will prefer to go without it rather than put up with poor quality or gross rudeness.

(iii) The third way is a combination of failure to keep track of market developments (absence of market intelligence) and failure to keep making small changes in product and process for constant improvements. These can be in the form of improvement in the quality of the product as well as reduction in the cost of production. Excuses like the ones offered by the foodstuff maker, Vishwakarma, are a part of this syndrome. He knows what the market wants and yet he fails to introduce necessary changes in his product. And there are some others who do not even bother to find out what the market wants.

Are you next in line?

The fundamental question is whether you are at all complacent about your products and customers, believing that you can expect to sell them in undiminishing quantity to the same customers. The questions in Box 4.1 may perhaps help you to avoid this blunder and its ill-effects. I must caution you that marketing myopia is a very complex phenomenon and not all its dimensions are captured by the following questions. They only help you escape the more obvious signs.

BOX 4.1
**Questions to assess the soundness of
your marketing practices**

1. *When you receive a complaint from the customer regarding your product, what do you usually do?*

The responses in increasing order of sound marketing practice are:
☐ Just ignore the complaint;
☐ Call for details from the customer by ringing him up or writing to him;
☐ Send someone to visit him and understand from him the nature of the complaint;
☐ Replace the impugned goods irrespective first, get the lot back and analyse the causes of the problems.

2. *When a customer switches from you to another supplier, what do you do?*

☐ Tell yourself that the fellow must be getting it cheaper by a couple of rupees from your competitor and hence fight with the competitor for stealing your customer;
☐ Right away reduce the price by a few per cent and try to get the customer back on price basis alone;
☐ Talk to the customer about the reasons for the switch; and
☐ Carefully study the package of product and services offered by the competitor and try to understand the differences.

3. *How carefully have you personally understood the technical parameters defining quality of your product? How often do you pursue issues of quality with your managers, workers or staff?*

☐ You know the parameters but have no equipment for testing your product on them. You simply rely on your workers' skill for quality.
☐ You have at least the inexpensive testing equipment, carry out some of these tests once in a while mainly to make your workers feel that they are being supervised.
☐ You have all the necessary equipment and can personally carry out all the tests. But the firm maintains no batch-wise records of quality and tests are done only when complaints are received.
☐ All the tests are regularly undertaken for each batch and the QC report is presented to you personally, and what is more, at times you go and do these tests yourself so that no one just fills up the forms.

4. *How much do you know about the competitors?*

☐ You know the family and feel sure that they will not undercut you; in fact both of you keep giving 'supporting quotations' in tenders of public enterprises.
☐ You know the names and addresses of all the makers of all the leading brands and also their sales network, prices, discounts and trade credits.
☐ You keep the most recent samples of each of the packing sizes which the competitors make, analyse the product for the requisite quality and constantly compare it with your own products.
☐ Through suppliers and others you know about the product and process developments being made by the competitors even before they are fully implemented.

5. *How much do you know about your final customers and what they want?*

☐ Nothing at all, as you sell your products through distributors and you do not know the direct users at all.

□ You know broadly who these users are and also the use to which they put your product. But you do not maintain routine contacts with them.
□ You know the direct users well. You know the purchasing pattern, consumer behaviour, etc., and your knowledge comes from the dealers who sell your goods.
□ You keep tabs on direct users regularly and keep introducing changes in the product whenever you detect changing preferences.

BLUNDER 7: Hiring employees for reasons other than their competence

Description of the cases

Again I shall give a series of illustrations for this blunder.

1. Gupta is engaged in the manufacture of a range of sports goods which is regularly exported. He was talking to me about how this young chap Rahul who had joined him a year ago was a useless guy.

'I pay him well enough for his qualifications. After all, who will pay this ordinary B. Com. more than three thousand? Then I give him all the expenses he incurs on travel. But still, he was unable to prevent four duty-drawback cases from lapsing.'

He told me some more about his business. The manufacturing process needs many materials on which customs or excise duties and other taxes are required to be paid. When Gupta exports the materials, he becomes eligible for a drawback on these duties and taxes. Gupta has to follow up quite intensively with the concerned department for this purpose.

The typical cycle of one drawback operation is that he must get a certificate from the company which actually exports, though in Gupta's name, then he must get it countersigned by the SSIDC or the Nigam, and armed with these loads of papers with large rubber stamps affixed all over, go to the concerned department.

In a year Gupta sends some three dozen consignments. So this is done three dozen times. The value of each of the drawback is about a lakh of rupees. The exporting company is in Bombay, some 900 km away from where he is, the SSIDC and the Nigam as well as the concerned department in Allahabad, 80 km in the opposite direction.

This boy Rahul is a weakling, whom Gupta hired because his father came and pleaded with him. Gupta was cocksure that the boy would sit when he was told to and stand otherwise. That boy was unable to negotiate with the officers of the company or the SSIDC or the Nigam in getting things done quickly. He was scared of so much as giving them a cup of tea. He was not sure what the boss would say. He could not learn from the repeated efforts for devising any systems. At the sign of the first problem, he would rush to Gupta for advice.

Gupta told me (after knowing that I was an MBA myself), 'I talked to one MBA for hiring him. Oh God, you fellows think the earth of yourself. He has worked only for a year but asked for a salary of Rs 8,000 per month and said he will travel only by taxi to Delhi and may be even by air to Bombay. You know, even now I go to Delhi only by an AC bus. I myself take only ten thousand rupees home every month, and this boy wants eight! The MBA spoke in a language I could not understand and said he would start selling performance and even exporting others' stuff as in the export business there are more treasury profits than trading margins. I thought and decided that on the whole that MBA was not to be hired. He is so uppish already, soon he may start running my whole place and then what shall I do'?

2. Rajesh makes some mechanical components and also does reconditioning of heavy parts. The buyers are quite fussy about the quality of the components and reject them at the first sign of fall from expected standards. The firm started at first when Rajesh and his brother themselves used to work on the machines. Being well trained machinists and also owners, they never had the problem of quality verification or correctness of processes.

As the business expanded gradually, Rajesh hired people slowly, one at a time. He would train one fellow fully and when he began doing a good job, hire another and so on. Usually these boys were all-purpose workers. They were unskilled, poor and desperate for a job. As against the minimum wage of Rs 38 per day, they would accept just Rs 500 per month as they were hungry, unemployed and without hope.

They could do just what they were told and were absolutely out of their depth when faced with a situation for which they had been given no instructions. Since these workers have been with Rajesh for a few years now he feels bound to them as they have helped him in his hour of need. At the same time, he cannot hire fresh, qualified and skilled people because of space and financial constraints. He now finds the old boys quite inadequate for the jobs. He feels that they are holding him back.

3. The third case could be about almost any one of you. Pansari started his industry five years ago. He was virtually all the firm had: he got the orders, spent hours in the factory supervising production, ran around to organise the truck for dispatching the goods, handled the dealings with the bank, prepared the bills and chased on payments with the buyers.

Then soon he came in the sales tax-payer category and later in the excise duty-payable category. He just could not manage to do all the paperwork himself and yet run the factory. Fortunately, his neighbour's nephew was looking for a job. The lad was enthusiastic, honest and completely trustworthy—just what Pansari wanted. He was also doing Commerce and due to his father's health, was quite hard up.

Pansari hired him at Rs 1,000 per month. The boy first started taking care of the accounts, then started handling the bank and taking care of the sales tax and even excise returns. Pansari was very happy.

One day his C.A. came screaming and foaming at the mouth. It appeared that the boy had goofed up somewhere and caused a loss of some Rs 11,000 through excess payment. The C.A. said that most of the entries made in the account books were wrong, that on a large number of bills too much tax was paid and that it would take his articles some two weeks to sort the whole mess. The C.A. told Pansari that he must look through every entry made by this boy and check everything he did, for the boy's mistakes could cost him dear.

Pansari was mad and wanted to throw out the boy for his

incompetence. The boy cried. In the evening the boy's mother came and touched his feet and cried buckets. ('The whole household depends on his job, his father has been suffering for six months and we have to spend so much on medicines. I have started cooking in two-three houses to support the family. Please, sir, we will all starve if he is sacked'—and so on.)

Pansari's heart melted and he allowed the boy to stay on. Now Pansari has started doing the accounts, going to the bank and all the rest. For a while he cannot sack the boy, nor can he afford to lose another Rs 11,000. Pansari now finds that it takes him more time to patiently correct all the mistakes made by this boy than it did for him to do the work himself.

What was the entrepreneurs' rationale?

The mistake being discussed is *hiring many cheap employees and that too for reasons other than related to their competence, rather than few competent but more expensive employees.* For the sake of convenient explanation, let me call these cheap employees Harirams. (This of course is a spoof on the Hariram and the laughable jailer of the famous film '*Sholay*', for reasons that will soon become clear.)

The rationale of the entrepreneurs follows more or less the same pattern. There are several shades to it and different factors contribute to it. In the first place, entrepreneurs tend to avoid hiring any one at all. They are scared of adding to their overheads. An employee is a very visible form of overhead expenses.

Then, too, they would rather not hire someone who is from the same social stratum as their own. It is mainly because they find it difficult to assume the responsibility of supporting the employee's family, when they feel that their own firm is just about making two ends meet.

Second, they find it easier to hire the weak and the defenceless Hariram rather than a capable and self-assured person. Qualified and competent persons, particularly from the same social status as the entrepreneur, are bound to demand the treatment of an equal. The entrepreneur in his new role of the boss finds adjustment to the new concept of equality with an employee difficult.

However, the weak, ill-trained and unskilled Hariram tends to be very submissive. He never challenges what the boss asks him to do. He is also very quick with praise and soothing talk. Who does not like sycophancy?

Third, the entrepreneur tends to associate power/status/importance, etc., far too strongly with salary. He feels that facilities and expenses given to an employee are major 'favours' to him. A well-paid employee is not necessarily more powerful. If the entrepreneur himself goes standing in a bus to Delhi, as Gupta was fond of doing, it is because the surplus saved accrues to him. Nothing of the kind is happening to the employee. To expect him to put up with unnecessary discomfort and yet perform well, without giving him any share in surpluses, is basically wrong and untenable.

In the fourth place, entrepreneurs tend to have a fear of the professional. The professionals appear to them to be power hungry and threatening competitors. The hidden and inarticulate fear is that in some matters the professional may actually know better and then the entrepreneur will not be able to boss around so much. They thus feel the erosion of authority. This too is quite a misconception. The professional is only an employee and he will seldom overstep his position if he is any good.

Hiring a weak, defenceless, helpless and needy person like Hariram is very comforting for several reasons. In the first place, Hariram will always remain in deep obligations and be servile. That helps psychologically as the entrepreneur does not feel threatened. He has already earned deep gratitude from Hariram's needy family and hence gets a lot of social respect, standing and legitimacy.

Above all, Hariram is incompetent but not wholly useless. He does manage to do some things at least. All said and done, he is of some help. At times a lot of help as he willingly takes care of all the shady deals, cash transactions, bribing, reaching beer crates to the bank manager and so on. Later on, this Hariram starts being the trusted man of the boss for keeping an eye on others. (Do you now spot shades of Hariram and the jailer from *Sholay?*)

Why is this a blunder?

The reason this is a blunder is that though the cheap employee appears to save on salary and benefits, he costs a lot in terms of:

- Loss of managerial time in repeated corrections, elaborate explanations and detailed instructions which have to be given to him;
- Plain incompetence leading to loss of materials, time, orders and even money;
- Loss of opportunities; and finally
- When this mistake is repeated several times as many entrepreneurs are wont to, promising and good persons simply boycott the firm. The last happens because the whole pack of Harirams start ganging up after a while. They all know the entrepreneur and his family very well. Often they do some personal errands as well—*'Munne ko school chhod aana Hariram!'* (Drop the child to school, Hariram!).

When Harirams become firmly entrenched, they start kitchen politics of a most irritating kind. They start ganging up against competent and professional newcomers and indulge in rumour mongering, bickering and even plain falsehood.

If—God forbid (but entrepreneurs do not)—the entrepreneur's wife (*bhabhiji*) or mother (*maaji*) is seen to be on very matronly terms with these fellows and also taking active part in the business, the professional lasts only a few months. He cannot stand this mixing of kitchen politics with organisational work.

The entrepreneur cannot understand the professional's stand-offish behaviour. ('These Harirams are *my* people. They all regard me as their brother and come to me even with their personal problems. Only that MBA stands away scowling. Oh, these professionals are no good!' Does this sound familiar?)

And after the professionals have generally given up your organisation as a dead loss, you start becoming defensive. A new rationalisation comes to fore: *'Are sahab yeh naye chhokre to aate hi nahin hai,* or *aaye bhi to tikte nahin, chahe kitana paisa do inhe!'* (Oh, these new fellows just do not join me and if at all they join, they do not stay for long, irrespective of what you pay them.) In any case it would be far better to hire good fellows and pay them well, generate more surpluses and simply give a dole to all the Harirams. Harirams and the organisation are both better helped if the charity and the employment are kept separate.

When governments mix social objectives and business, economists as well as industrialists are fond of giving the following bit of advice:

> *Let all subsidies be direct and open, for all hidden subsidies also tend to hide incompetence, inefficiency and even corruption.*

In this regard, what is true of governments is also true of entrepreneurs.

When does it hit you?

As usual, these mistakes begin to haunt the entrepreneur when he is attempting to put his firm on a path of growth. By this stage, the urge to continue to oblige poor relations has usually subsided and ambition has taken over. The entrepreneur realises that poor Hariram can neither be sacked nor be put to any particular use.

The entrepreneur may want to expand by establishing relations with new customers in large cities or deal with other important matters and persons. He wants some, if not all, of the new tasks to be handled by competent staff. Very possibly, he is of middle-age now and cannot stand too much travel and strain.

Many such customers and important persons demand greater technical knowledge and more polished appearance and manners from the representatives of the firm than what Hariram can give. After all, Hariram is from a poor family, has had no advantage of a good education and is capable of saying virtually nothing except *banji* to the *Bade Bhai Sahib*.

Hariram can seldom clinch a deal by competently engaging the potential buyer at a technical level or taking on-the-spot decisions on small matters. So he keeps saying, *'Ye to bade bhai batayenge'* (The boss will tell you this.) After one or two *'Woh to bade bhai batayenge!'* from him the potential buyer gets tired and sends him away.

What are the alternatives to this employment policy?

The most preferred alternative is to wait as long as you can before you hire an employee. When you are sure that you need one for a well-identified set of tasks and that you can afford to pay a good salary for a competent person, then hire. Do not hire in a hurry. Keep looking and pick up some one you feel is really good. Do not stint while fixing his salary. Give him two hundred *more* than what he asks. And then load him with work, be strict in demanding performance and generous in appreciating work.

BOX 4.2
Are you the comic jailer of your Harirams?
Assessing how close you are to Blunder 7.

1. *How long does an average new employee, particularly in technically or managerially important categories, last in your firm?*

Any thing less than a year indicates that Harirams have now gained strength.

2. *Do your employees protest at the fact that you do not follow the labour laws? (It is quite likely that you are defaulting either on the Minimum Wages Act, Payment of Bonus, ESIS, PF or some thing. Pitifully few of the small-industry owners abide by all the labour laws.)*

If your employees do not protest but are, in fact, grateful to have been hired, it indicates that you have been hiring potential Harirams.

3. *How frequently does any one of your staff and employees tell you that you are wrong?*

It is possible that the employees suggest their disagreement with you in an indirect and subtle manner but you are too insensitive to notice it. After all one always beats around the bush while arguing with the boss, and more so if one is certain that he is wrong. So be on your guard and try to understand what they mean.

If the answer is that no one ever tells you even politely when you are wrong, sack the lot and hire new fellows. No one, not even you can always be right. More importantly, this is dangerous because it indicates that you really have a pack of sycophants around you. You will be stunted because of complacence.

Questions to be answered for every employee:

1. *How was this person hired?*

☐ Through a genuine process of search and interview;
☐ Because his father, the Excise (or Sales Tax or the Nigam or the SSIDC or the SEB) officer came to meet you asking for a job for his son (what is quite pardonably called the 'environmental pressure case');
☐ Because your mother or wife said the boy's family needed help;
☐ Because at that time, no one else seemed willing to work for the salary you were willing to give.

The last two answers indicate problem cases. The second case is eminently sackable, if found useless and if the father has been transferred.

2. *Do you think this person can earn as much as you pay him outside?*

☐ Oh, certainly, perhaps much more;
☐ Just about;
☐ No way. No one will look at him.

The last two answers indicate problems.

3. *How often do you or your family ask this chap to do some thing (however small and silly it may be) for the family?*

☐ Virtually never, how can we? He is such a senior officer.
☐ Only occasionally, when it is to be done in the area where he stays.

> - ☐ About once a week.
> - ☐ Almost every day, as he is more or less a family member anyway.
>
> The last two answers indicate problems, unless the chap also has or is likely to have an equity stake in the firm.
>
> **4.** *How often does your mother or wife speak to you for giving something/helping this fellow in some way?*
>
> - ☐ Never, she hardly knows him personally.
> - ☐ Oh, she did last month once.
> - ☐ Quite often, and why not?
>
> The last answer is positively dangerous.

At times you have to suffer the Harirams of this world. It is virtually impossible to refuse to favour all the people who insist on sending seedy-looking, incompetent young persons for employment. Those who recommend may include your close relations, senior government officers, persons in a position to do you great favours or cause you big nuisance and so on. So when you must hire for reasons other than the employee's competence, ensure that you do not entrust any task of consequence to him. Let him just file junk mail or sort of clean the stables. Only when you are assured of his worth, give him something substantial to do. Have no compunction in sacking incompetent Harirams. You must first ensure your industry's sustained growth. Unless you are a multimillionaire, you need not presume that the burden of supporting the weak must be borne by you. Never permit sycophancy; remember, every sycophant is essentially a manipulator. Above all, do not collect too many Harirams.

Are you next in line?

This mistake is both very obvious and very difficult to accept and realise. You may like to list all the employees in his firm, right from the peon to the engineers. I would suggest that he should try and calmly ask himself the questions given in Box 4.2. He may answer questions 1 through 4 about each one of these employees individually. Questions 1 through 3 are general and may be answered for the whole group.

BLUNDER 8: Unrealistic or faulty project planning

This is naturally of special relevance to the would-be entrepreneurs as well as those of you who are setting up a new project.

Description of the cases

1. Praveen manufactures sheets which are used by some industries in Khede. They in turn sell the products based on the sheets to the Nigam. The demand pattern of Nigam is highly seasonal. It needs a lot of material from October to March but virtually nothing from April to September. Consequently the industries in Khede also have an intensely seasonal operations pattern. They operate from August to February and are more or less dormant from March onwards.

It is important for suppliers to these industries, such as Praveen, to be able to maximise production and sales between July and January, which is the time during which materials are ordered and expected. Praveen set up his factory in the year 1986. It was scheduled to go on stream in September 1986, which it did.

However, as is usual, after trial runs were taken, some snags cropped up and it took another three months to eventually start commercial operations. That meant beginning of December. Praveen had to first make people try out his product. Virtually no commercial sales occurred in the 1986 financial year.

The next year was a recession year for the entire industry and orders for sheets were at half the normal level. Again, a new player like Praveen had to take a beating in order quantities as well as price. As a result, for the first two years Praveen made no cash profit. In fact, the book losses were substantial. The interest amounts on at least the working capital had to be paid. The liquidity suffered as a result. Since he had missed two consecutive years for sales, his projections went haywire and the firm reached the somewhat unenviable level of neither being healthy nor utterly sick.

A similar case is described in Box 4.3 below.

BOX 4.3

The ignoble story of an explosive company

This is the description of a company, somewhat larger than the other enterprises being described. It made explosives which were used in highly specialised applications and could lead to dangerous accidents if mishandled.

As a result, there were very severe tests to be performed before the relevant departments could certify that the explosives produced in the factory were safe enough to be transported and used in the applications for which they were required. The testing procedures concerned specifically required storage of the product for some time to see the extent of deterioration and safety in storage.

The tests were required of all the manufacturers, but for a factory about to be set up, the requirements were tougher and more thorough. The project report expected the sales to commence from the very first year of starting operations. Based on that projection the company had taken loans for working capital, arranged for marketing network, etc. The severe testing requirements in reality took over ten months during which time not one gramme of explosives could be sold. The production was, however, started in right earnest as the clearances always appeared very close. So the finished goods inventory was large.

Over and above this, the department required certain changes in the lay-out of the storage and hence a substantial amount of money had to be spent on that. Again, interest amounts had to be paid. The result was that the company started with very poor liquidity and scarce manoeuvrability in the market. It took six years for the company to come out of the situation caused by the initial faltering and show profits.

What was the entrepreneurs' rationale?

The rationale in both the cases is that what happened is not according to design at all; it is simply one of those things one failed to anticipate while planning the project.

They retrospectively agree that the financing of the project should have included a component for taking care of loss of liquidity arising out of such contingency. *The basic cause of the trouble was that in neither case had the project plan taken into account the fact that due to reasons of seasonality or tight regulation, there would be huge pile up of materials produced but unsold in the first year.* Neither of the two causes was sudden or unexpected. They should have been expected. Hence the blunder is of improper planning.

Thus, the working capital was all used up without generating any sales. And that would erode liquidity in any case. In fact, it would not at all be surprising if one were to discover that starting trouble due to problems with technology (happened to, for example, Lactose India), seasonality or regulation (illustrated above) or raw materials (particularly for those who depend on imported or some special raw materials) were the chief causes of sickness in new industries.

Why is it a blunder?

This blunder represents a set of mistakes which occur at the project planning and implementation stage. The basic cause is inadequate coordination between project implementation (including commissioning of fully commercial operations) and use of funds.

Mistakes either occur in not anticipating the snags of the above kind or in predicting the effect of seasonality of market on commercial performance in the initial years. It is to be realised that in the initial years of operation, the firm is particularly ill-equipped to handle things like missing the peak season, and long gestation period for maturing sales.

It has just sufficient working capital to see through operations if they run normally. No operating cash surpluses have accumulated. Its market standing is yet to be built. Hence, virtually all purchases are on ready-payment basis. Market establishment as well as product promotion are known to cause a drain on cash.

When does it hit you?

This particular mistake hurts the entrepreneur only in the very initial stages of his project, and perhaps at the beginning of any new project he undertakes.

The reason I have not expanded on this mistake is simple. An industry can commit it only once. This is unlike all the earlier mistakes, all of which can be committed any time and over and over again. The only way to avoid this mistake is to first find out every possible reason why the project will not be able to become commercially operational even after commissioning of the factory. Then one must start working on the causes, moving applications, obtaining clearances, etc., in advance. In any case one must very clearly budget for an operational loss of a sizeable magnitude for the first year for all projects whose markets are seasonal or subject to regulations.

Summary of the typical Blunders

S.No.	Action in question	Sources of motivation	When OK and for whom	Set of problems	How to circumvent
1.	Excessive or exclusive dependence on one buyer	A. Social kinship or past association B. Reducing marketing hassles C. Initial support for financing trade	If you have strong family/social links If dependence is mutual	Wide fluctuation in demand Payment delays Ignorance of customers needs	Develop alternate buyers/products or channels
2.	Expanding fixed assets before providing for working capital	A. Being able to garner more market share B. Technological upgradation	Never recommended	Liquidity crunch Loss of market standing Bankruptcy Liquidity crunch	To avoid completely
3.	Borrowing in cash market for stocking up materials	A. Seasonal price variations	For those whose financial leverage is low	Reduction in formal business	To simultaneously hedge in final product
4.	Doing informal business	A. Generating cash for bribes and speed money	Only to a small extent to meet genuine cash needs	Remaining under a constant threat	Maximising formal business

Table contd.

S.No.	Action in question	Sources of motivation	When OK and for whom	Set of problems	How to circumvent
		B. Expanding personal wealth	Never more than 25% of turnover	Absence of solidity in formal accounts Shady image	
5.	Spawning too many firms	A. Staying in a category which has smaller binding staff expenses	Only if you have no desire to make it big	All firms remain small figures in on books	Ensure that a core firm shows solid figures in accounts
		B. Tax avoidance			
		C Achieving flexibility in bookkeeping	Where each small firm has enough potential to grow		
		D. Ensuring that each offspring has an independent business to manage			
6.	Marketing myopia (selling whatever one makes rather than making what is desired by customers)	A. Hangover of shortage economy	Those with very small operations	Losing touch with buyers	Avoid Blunder 1
		B. Avoiding marketing overheads.	Those who have unbeatable advantage of space/uniqueness of features	Inability to grasp big opportunities Low realisations	Engage in constant and systematic market monitoring Pay attention to quality

7.	Hiring employees for reasons other than competence	A. Social pressures to accommodate boys	Not recommended except when social pressures are very strong	Permanently impairing organisational ability	Keep social subsidy explicit
		B. Distrust and fear of qualified persons		Kitchen cabinet effect deters good persons from joining firm sycophancy culture	If you must hire low competence staff ensure continuous skill improvement
		C. Minimising wage costs		Expensive mistake of employees	Keep work and family matters separate
8.	Unrealistic project planning (leading to delayed sales and blocked liquidity)	Usually by default		Firm goes into red and stays there.	

PART THREE

Managing it Right

So far I have done two things. In the first place I have tried to tell you what this liberalisation is going to do to the small-scale enterprises, and second, I have tried to argue that growth is not a matter of choice or ambition any more, but simply an imperative for survival.

The markets are becoming more competitive and the parameters of competition are changing. You may well argue that in this situation it is not enough to simply point out the mistakes you ought to avoid. You have also got to be helped positively, by assisting you in moving towards the right decisions. Of course, all free advice should be utterly disregarded because it is often irresponsible advice. Therefore, without any intention of offering specific, free advice but simply to make my book complete, I offer some positive comments in this part.

In Chapter 5, I shall deal with key concepts in managing finances which will be useful to you. In Chapter 6, I explain the simple framework used by management pundits to talk about competition and the various bases for competing in the newly developing markets. In Chapter 7, I talk of three general options in taking a stance in the market. Then in Chapter 8, I shall deal the dimensions of growth: management of sales growth, matching it with asset expansion, managing the finances needed, and management of quality. Chapter 9 shall take up the crucial organisational and human resource issues involved in the pangs of growth. Finally, I end the book by pointing out some more banana skins on which you can slip, as well as tell you how and why to avoid getting ensnared by glib-talking fair-weather consultants.

5

How Best to Manage Your Finances

I deal with three crucial aspects of financial management in this chapter. The first is the assessment of the actual working capital need of your business given the existing business situation, profit opportunities and your desires. The second is the nature of risky financing as reflected in high leverage. Finally, I take up the matter of the various ways, as they exist now, of raising additional finances, their advantages and disadvantages.

Assessing the level of working capital you need

In the first place, it is necessary that you clearly differentiate between assessing the need for working capital and assessing the need for raising your own funds for the purpose. For running your business smoothly you need, say Rs 20 lakh, apart from the investment needed in plant and machinery. If this calculation is right and if you have Rs 20 lakh, the business will run smoothly whether you have put Rs 20 lakh of personal money, bank loan or cash borrowing from a shark.

In the last two cases, out-of-pocket financial cost will be larger. In the first case, the opportunity cost will be higher. And naturally, the leverage of the firm will be different as we shall see below. These parameters affect the mode of financing, not the level of funds needed.

Working capital is defined as the excess of current assets over current liabilities. Current liabilities include the money you owe to outsiders in the short term, as well as charges, levies, installments and payments which fall due in the short term. Current assets include payments you expect to receive in the short term and the stocks of materials and finished goods which you hold. When we say that the working capital need is large, it means that you owe less money in the short term to outsiders than you are likely to receive. (I must confess that accounting and finance were never my favourite subjects and I can now see why!) This way of understanding the term working capital is not the most appropriate or even practical. In a way, this way one confuses the need for working capital and the ways to raise it.

Assessing the need

I suggest a way of assessing the working capital need. This is conventionally called the 'pipeline' method of calculating the level of working capital. At the core of this method lies the following question:

If starting from the stage of raw materials to the stage of getting payments for finished goods we count as one cycle, what is the length of this working cycle?

It is presumed that the payments for finished goods received are being ploughed back in the business and being used to buy materials. Thus, the entrepreneur must provide money only for this pipeline period. The amount is calculated by using what we know about the process, such as when is which material needed. Basic raw material is needed right at the beginning, packing materials are needed only when the production is ready, excise duty is to be paid just on the day of dispatching the materials, etc.

One also has to provide some more money for taking care of wages, salaries, telephone, electricity, petrol, postage, courier, etc. One can and should become quite precise in answering this question as only then one's calculations will be right. This also helps you to automatically identify various ways of generating finances for the working capital. This process is illustrated with the help of an example from a super-enamelled wire unit described in Box 5.1.

BOX 5.1
Assessing the working capital needed for a SE copper wire unit of capacity one tonne per day

This unit makes Super-Enamelled (SE) copper wire. The copper wire rods are available in Bombay the unit is in Akola. After purchase, the wire rods have to be annealed in a rolling mill in Bombay. Then they are transported to Akola. It takes the annealed wire rods one week to reach Akola from the date of delivery of basic rods. Then the process of SE wire making begins.

Wire rods are cleaned or pickled with mild acid. For this they are simply immersed in the pickling tank for half a day. The wire rods are then pre-drawn to reduce their diameter. Then the wire drawing is done. The time required for wire drawing depends on the thickness of the wire being produced. Thicker wires need only a single pass and hence are drawn quickly. Thinner wires need two passes and hence take double the time.

The drawn wires are then enamelled by passing them through enamelling machines. Enamelled wires are wound on wooden spools, tested for quality, packed and become ready for dispatch. As a typical order includes several types of wires, it takes some time to assemble all the types before sending the lot. Acid, enamels, chemicals, etc., are needed for this process apart, of course, from the power, human labour and heating oils.

On an average, it takes one week for wires drawn from wire rods to be dispatched. In other words, the stock of in-process materials is about a week. The wires are sold to traders in Vidarbha. The time for the wires to reach them is about three days from dispatch. They send the demand draft after an average of two weeks after receiving the wire; the transit and realisation of the drafts take on an average one week.

To ensure continuous running of the factory, adequate stocks of materials should be available all the time. Given the value of materials, distances from the supplier involved and the suppliers' reliability, the unit must keep a stock of wire rods for one week and wooden spools, chemicals and resins for one month. The unit also needs to keep about Rs 5 lakh as bank balance for making routine expenses like payments for wages, electricity, and freight.

The length of the working cycle in the case of a super-enamelled wire unit is roughly estimated below:
- Time between buying wire rods and receiving them in the factory: one week
- Time for processing: one week
- Time for transit of goods to buyers: three days
- Average trade credit: two weeks
- Time for transit and realisation of payments: one week
  Total: five-and-a-half weeks

If the daily capacity is manufacture of one metric tonne of SE wires, then the total working capital that is needed just for this pipeline is equivalent to 38 tonnes of copper! As copper is sold at about Rs 130 per kg, this means that the working capital needed is approximately Rs 50 lakh plus some more for holding the stocks of materials. If you provide for this kind of money for the factory, you can run it very well as long as the assumptions were right.

Let us refine the calculation. Let us assume that the basic copper price is Rs 130 per kg. At one MT per day, for one week, the copper needed is seven tonnes costing Rs 9.1 lakh. Let us assume the value addition in all subsequent stages and see how the working capital need emerges. This is shown in Table 5.1.

TABLE 5.1: Assessing Working Capital Needed for the Pipeline Period

Stage	Length in weeks	Unit value as % of copper	Total money blocked (Rupees lakh)
Receipt of wire rods	one	100	9.1
Processing	one	116	10.6
Dispatch	half	140	6.4
Trade credit	two	142	25.8
Recovery of payment	one	143	13.0
Total	five-and-a-half		64.9

One will have to add the moneys needed for safety stock as well as the five lakh needed for making routine payments. The stock of copper is needed for one week. The other materials cost just 13 per cent of copper value and one needs to have them for a month. Thus, the raw material stocks are valued at Rs 14 lakh (Rs 9.1 lakh for copper and Rs 5 lakh for other materials).

The total working capital needed will be Rs 65 lakh for the pipeline, Rs 14 lakh for safety stocks and Rs 5 lakh for safety bank balance, i.e., Rs 84 lakh in all.

How to generate finances

It is presumed, of course, that all these time estimates for various processes are the shortest times possible. If it were possible to manage with only two days safety stock of copper or if one can get the copper delivered in three days instead of a week, then the working capital needed reduces. After assessing the most likely level of necessary working capital, one may provide for a little more than that to become comfortable in working. Then in reality one may start pruning the stocks, credit periods and so on. As usual one hopes for and tries for the best but is prepared for the worst.

When the questions regarding raising the level of working capital is concerned, the key question in raising the amount thus calculated is as follows:

At each of these stages of the pipeline, how much money will I have to put, how much can be reasonably expected from trade credits and how much will be needed from banks?

The associated question is, of course, what is the cost of getting trade credit. For example:

- Copper may be available on credit but only at two per cent per month;
- Chemicals and resin suppliers may give trade credits as a part of their sales policy;
- Local traders, i.e., those in Akola may be willing to accept part deliveries and hence the time for assembly of a lot may be saved;
- Some traders may be willing to pay in cash on delivery if they get a 1 per cent cash discount;
- Payment of sales tax can be deferred if one pays the interest at 24 per cent per annum; and so on.

The financial costs of strategies inherent in all five cases are explicit, but the management costs are not so. These have been elaborated in the discussion on Blunder 3 and need not be repeated here. Suffice it to say that these become very severe for people who adopt these strategies because they do not have money with them.

While the above example illustrates the process to be used for calculation of working capital for the pipeline, the steps are explicitly stated in Table 5.2.

TABLE 5.2: Steps for Assessing the Length of the Operating Cycle and the Working Capital for the Pipeline

S.No.	Stage	Likely procedure	Value addition	Expected time	Credit availability
1.	Key raw material purchase and its transport to factory	Advance payment, spot payment, trade credit	Nil	X1 days	Y/N @1% pm
2.	Safety stock of key raw materials	NA	Nil	X2 days	NA
3.	Processing	NA	V1% of material cost	X3 days	NA
4.	Storage period of finished goods		V2% of material cost	X4 days	
5.	Trade inventories		V3% of material cost	X5 days	Trade financing
6.	Trade credit		V3% of material cost	X6 days	Spot Payments

In this way, the length of the pipeline is (X1+X2+X3+X4+X5+X6). You will make calculations similar to those in Table 5.1. Start with unit value of raw material, and the expected quantum to be consumed per day. At each stage, multiply the per day consumption by the total value (that is, [100+V1] per cent for stage 3, [100+V2] for stage 4, etc.) and by the number of days in that stage. Cumulate all these and you will get the total working capital needed for the pipeline. Then you will have to add the minimum cash balance you want in the bank account for taking care of wages, freight, postage and other urgent costs.

You would understand that not each one of the steps may be applicable for each of the industrial units. Some may be able to buy raw materials on credit, some may pay on delivery and some may have to pay in advance. It will depend both on the type of industry you are in as well as the market conditions in it. If you are located near the raw material supplier, you could manage with raw material stock of just a week; or else you may need to stock it for longer duration. Some industries must store the finished goods for sometime before dispatching it, for technical reasons. Some may have to send it 'fresh from the oven'. Some of you may have to give trade credits. Some may arrange for a distributor to finance all trade inventories and credits.

Understanding and using leverage

The term leverage comes from the original principle of lever, in which one increases the effectiveness of one's efforts by using a simple lever. Thus leveraging means devising ways to magnify the effect.

Fixed and variable costs

The concept of leverage is of fundamental importance to the small industry, especially at its growth phase. Generally, leverage arises when a fixed cost is incurred but it generates only uncertain revenues thus making the residue very variable.

To understand all the ramifications of the concept of leverage, it is important to first study the concepts of fixed and variable costs. In the total business processes of procurement of materials, manufacture of the product, its marketing and distribution some costs are fixed and some change with the volume of business.

Strictly speaking, nothing is fixed forever; it is fixed only in a certain range. Thus, land rent for the industrial plot you have leased from the SIDC is about the most fixed you can go. But even that will vary (in some awkward relation to production volume) when you produce more than the capacity of the existing factory. The term *fixed cost* refers to those costs which do not change within a certain range of production and certainly do not change directly on a *per unit basis*.

Thus, the peak load or demand charge for your electric connection changes only when you ask for higher peak load. Then again it changes not on the basis of per unit of your production. Continuing with this live-wire discussion, electricity used for general lighting, fans, etc., in your factory does not change on a per unit (of your production) basis. These are then fixed costs.

On the other hand, material used for production changes on a per unit of sale basis. So does the direct labour use, running of drive motors, consumption of packaging materials and so on. Such costs which do vary with the level of production on a per unit basis are called *variable costs*. (There is always something in between such as lubricants, minor spares, and repairs and maintenance for machines which vary with the volume of sales, but not strictly on a per unit basis. These are called semi-variable costs, but you can ignore this complication for the moment.)

Further, some costs arise out of operations and no matter what you wished, they are absolutely required if you are to be in business. Thus, if you want to manufacture coolers, some fabrication equipment is necessary, so are some fixed costs. Coolers need mild steel sheets, welding electrodes, grass screens, motors, pumps and so on. As a result, material costs are incurred. All these are costs of operations or *operating costs*, some of which are fixed and some variable.

But there are other costs which are purely financial in nature and depend upon how you have obtained the necessary capital, how you are using it and how you are accounting for it. If, for example, you have sunk in a lot of your money in the business, there will be much less paid-out-interest costs involved. But if you have had to borrow in the cash market, a lot of interest cost is involved. Similarly, if you use Written Down Value method for depreciation (do not ask me what this is, ask your C.A.), then your depreciation charge is likely to be higher in the initial years.

The costs of running the business which arise because of your decision regarding source, use and accounting of finance are called *financial costs*. While they are as important as operating costs, they are (theoretically) amenable to much greater manipulation at your choice. Some financial costs are fixed and some variable. Thus, the working capital required and consequently the interest paid by you to the bank or to the shark for working capital finance depend on your level of business (as well as your efficiency in managing the working capital). Hence the interest on working capital is a variable cost. But interest on the loan for plant and machinery taken from the SSIDC or the bank is fixed irrespective. You have to pay the same interest whether you use 5 per cent of your capacity or 100 per cent. It is, thus, a fixed cost.

Gross profit is a term used to illustrate the difference between net sales realisation and the variable costs of your sales. Every businessman knows the concept of break-even level of sales, which is the one where the gross profit equals the fixed cost burden. When the break-even volume is a high proportion of capacity to manufacture, it makes life very troublesome. This realisation makes most Indian businessmen choose inexpensive and hence technologically backward production machinery.

Some capital-intensive manufacturing lines have inherently very high break-even volumes. Usually, in these lines the manufacturing value addition is sizeable. On the other hand, in agro-industries and many other lines the value addition is small, the industry is not capital intensive and break-even volumes are also low. These lines are almost like trading.

Rather than getting cowed down by these concepts, it is important to understand the spirit behind them and to apply them to one's situation. For example, perhaps the capital intensity in a particular line is high and hence you think it is too risky. It still does not mean that you should not enter it, may be the existing fellows are more than willing to do job work. By the job work route, you actually eliminate a majority of the fixed costs (but you also lose control on quality, priority and timing).

The operating profit (strictly defined, profit after meeting all operating costs, but before any financial costs) is gross profit less the fixed operating costs like salaries, welfare, etc. Operating Leverage (OL) is the ratio of percentage change in operating profit to percentage change in sales. Operationally,

$$OL = \frac{\text{\% change in profit before interest and tax (PBIT)}}{\text{\% change in sales}}$$

Naturally, the exact value of OL keeps varying as the level of sales changes and by itself is not very important. Generally, the higher the proportion of fixed costs in sales value, higher is the operating leverage. The significance of operating leverage is that it suggests the rapidity with which the firm could end up sinking below the break-even point. It points out the level of downward risk. Unfortunately, operating leverage is not a matter of too great a choice except wherever job work, wet lease with purely variable charges or similar options exist.

From operating profit, one has to remove the fixed financial costs and tax to arrive at Profit After Tax (PAT). Degree of Financial Leverage (FL) is the ratio of percentage change in PAT by percentage change in PBIT, i.e.

$$FL = \frac{\text{\% change in PAT}}{\text{\% change in PBIT}}$$

If the interest costs are very small owing to the almost complete internal financing of the facility, the PBIT and PAT will be nearly proportional, and the FL will be close to unity. That is the case of extreme conservatism. On the other hand, if the capital intensity is high and if all the fixed investment is from borrowed money, then FL will be very high.

Total Leverage (TL) is the product of OL and FL, i.e.,

$$TL = OL \times FL = \frac{\text{\% change in PAT}}{\text{\% change in sales volume}}$$

This total leverage sums up basically the degree of total downward risk associated with the firm. For example, when the sales volume drops by ten per cent, does the PAT turn negative or does it fall merely by 20 per cent? Naturally, the value of TL keeps varying as the sales volume moves away from the break-even point. Usually, it is good to consider the value of TL at the average capacity utilisation level of the industry. That will tell you what will happen if your firm performs a little below the industry level.

To illustrate these concepts, two examples are given, using

fictitious but realistic numbers. The sales volumes are assumed at industry capacity utilisation levels. These are shown in Table 5.3.

TABLE 5.3: Illustrative Examples of Break-even and Operating Leverage
(value in lakh rupees)

S.No.		Firm 1	Firm 2
1.	Industry	edible oil	texturised soya
2.	Capacity	5 MT per day	4 MT per day
3.	Investment	25 lakh	53 lakh
4.	Average sales	225	114
5.	Raw material	209	93
6.	Gross profit	16	21
7.	Overheads other than depreciation and interest	6	9
8.	Depreciation	1	4.3
9.	PBIT	9	7.7
	Interest on fixed capital (2:1 D/E ratio)	2.8	4.7
10.	PBT	6.2	3.0

In the edible oil line, the raw material cost is 93 per cent of sales value, while in the texturised soya line it is 81 per cent. Assuming these percentages, if the sales drop by ten per cent in both the cases, let us see the results in Table 5.4.

Obviously, the texturised soya line is more sensitive to changes in level of sales. Part of the reason for the high total leverage is that the soya unit is more capital intensive (the ratio of sales to fixed investment is just 2.15 for soya) than the edible oil unit (where this ratio is 9). Also, the assumed sales volume of Rs 114 lakh is already close to break-even of the soya unit at Rs 70 lakh. The sales volume of the edible oil line at Rs 225 lakh though a mere 30 per cent of capacity, is quite far from the break-even volume at Rs 100 lakh.

With high total leverage, the downward risk is higher as reflected in total leverage. Of course, the upward movement of profit is also equally high for soya. That is the whole temptation of leverage. Entrepreneurs are tempted to adopt high leverage strategy hoping that everything will work out the way they wish. I do not like this at all. Perhaps I am a born pessimist.

TABLE 5.4: Effect of Change in Sales Volume

	Edible oil	Texturised soya
Sales	202.5	102.6
Raw materials	188.3	83.1
Overheads	5.2	8.4
Depreciation	1	4.3
PBIT	8.0	6.8
Interest on fixed loan	2.8	4.7
PBT	5.2	2.1
Drop in sales	10%	10%
Drop in PBIT	11.1%	11.6%
Drop in PBT (same as drop in PAT)	16.1%	30%
Hence OL	1.11	1.16
FL	1.45	2.58
TL	1.61	3.0

The central point of understanding and using leverage is while your optimism keeps you thinking about the extra profit you will generate, the concept of leverage helps you properly assess the downward risk of your decision. Consider the decision of borrowing in the cash market for stocking up raw material. Like my friend Raghavan in Blunder 3, you think that it will give you so much extra sales, hence so much extra gross profit, extra net profit, etc. So he incurs a heavy fixed cost of cash interest. The moment some-thing goes wrong with the sales volume, the high fixed cost becomes a dead-weight capable of drowning him!

I would advise you to modify this concept to suit your special case. When assessing the impact of a financial burden, start by believing that you will be a good debtor and would always like to pay your liabilities in time. Keep looking at all possible outflows not directly connected with the sales level as fixed costs. These may even include things like periodic bribes which must be paid if your business is to run smoothly.

What you may like to include in these fixed costs for the

purpose of calculating leverage are: salaries, electricity bills, sales tax payments, all formal banking charges and interests on your CC/HYP or BD/BP loans, employee benefits, bribes, travel expenses and so on. Having done that, now calculate operating leverage, financial leverage and total leverage of your firm which will result from the decision which you are contemplating. Anything above 3 in the total leverage is risky.

Remember that your efforts are and can be only one part of the story of sales—and more importantly sales realisation. The other part has to do with things beyond your control: supply of auxiliary stuff like packing materials, behaviour of transportation and distribution chains, the number of market holidays, logistics of collection of money, and the honesty and promptitude of your dealers and retailers. For any one of these unexpected but likely reasons, the expected positive change in sales may not happen. Where does that leave you—with a whole lot of extra fixed liability and the leverage principle working inexorably but cruelly against you reducing your profits massively, perhaps pushing you into losses and worse still, causing an acute liquidity crunch? Is the game still worth playing? At least the proper use of this concept of leverage makes you take more rigorously thought-through decisions.

The same is indeed true for all the decisions which lead to Blunders 2, 3 and 4. The same principle is to be applied consistently and honestly for your own good. Blunder 2 tends to increase the total leverage in two ways. In the first place, by reducing the available finance for working capital, it makes more expensive borrowings necessary and hence reduces margins, increasing the leverage in general. Second, the decision also increases the (non-productive?) fixed costs. Blunder 4, namely the one in which business is done informally, has the effect of severely reducing formal turnover, often reducing formal ability to meet fixed costs. Only the desire to induce voluntary sickness can justify it, and I do hope you are not that sort of entrepreneur.

Different methods of raising finances

The discussion in this section is to indicate the range of options available to the entrepreneur, so that he is not compelled by his ignorance to borrow to his detriment in the cash market. The choice of a definite way of financing is to be made by the entrepreneur in the context of his specific circumstances.

Methods for reducing the level of borrowed working finance

1. Using hired facilities and equipment: Rather than buying equipment and facilities, you may simply hire them. Such things are possible for quite a few equipments such as computers, phones and vehicles. Not only do you save on the capital costs of these machines, you are also freed of the worry to maintain them. You may avoid the liabilities of staff becoming permanent and use the funds thus released to make your working capital base stronger. Naturally, your monthly expenses become higher. What happens is that the costs which would have become fixed costs otherwise, are converted into variable costs and hence leverage is reduced. The next stage is use of leased equipment.

2. Buying raw materials and services on credit: Every one tries to do this. What has to be ensured is that you get the best deal in terms of quality, delivery and price but still get a credit. The credit must be negotiated as a pure financial cost, at so many per cent a month. Never allow the credit charge to be included in the price, as that way you lose a bit of information on price and hence have lower bargaining power.

Some amount of discipline is required while following this policy. While you buy on credit, you must make it a habit of settling the bills on the due date. Stretched credits, if done repeatedly, will make your supplier lose faith in your word and hence you will get second-class treatment from him.

3. Offering attractive trade discounts for spot payments: Again this is a common strategy. The point is to use it only when working capital is becoming restrictive in raising volumes. Suppose you are selling your product at Rs 55 per kg and your costing assumes a built-in trade credit period of three weeks. If the normal interest rate assumed for your costing is 24 per cent, then you have assumed a cost of credit at 1.5 per cent.

The trick is to offer a little more than what it costs you, so that it is attractive to the buyer. In fact, if the working capital is restrictive and you are thinking of borrowing in the cash market at 2 per cent, then the real cost of credit is really 3.3 per cent (after adding the tax effect). Hence, you must be willing to offer a three per cent discount for spot payment.

You have to be careful here. Buyers are shrewd and try to take advantage of you. They will give you a cheque which may mean three to four days' credit in it, and sometimes their cheque may have to be presented more than once. If you are giving a liberal cash discount, insist on a payment in demand draft or banker's cheque so that you do get the money the same day.

4. Appointing a sole distributor: You may consider appointing a sole distributor, who will make spot payments to you and take care of the trade credit. This way you reduce the level of working finance needed by you. But there are several dangers in this method.

First of all, in becoming solely dependent on one distributor, you definitely risk Blunder 1. So you must have fall-back options or better still, three or four such distributors who will offer similar services.

Second, dependence on one distributor massively increases the moneys due from one party, if at all you extend credit to him. That is the danger sign. As long as he makes payments for every consignment on delivery, you are reasonably safe; but you know how it is. During holidays or times of a temporary cash crunch, you have to extend him some credit. And, of course, you also expect similar accommodation from him in your hour of need. Such accommodation then could become more a norm than an exception and suddenly you discover that one distributor owes you a substantial amount of money. You can neither afford to give him more material nor displease him!

Third, even assuming that he is paying in time, you do lose a measure of control on the market. You may not really know the prices he is charging to the buyers, what the buyers feel about the product and what is happening in the market-place. This could make you isolated.

5. Doing a job work or 'conversion': You should be clear that you are primarily interested in the manufacturing margin. If you are, then there is usually no harm in undertaking custom operations, conversion assignments or job work. In all these synonymous arrangements, the raw material is bought and given to the manufacturer by the buyer. The manufacturer undertakes the conversion or the job work and returns the finished goods and by-products to the buyer. He gets a conversion charge, to cover all his manufacturing costs and a bit of margin. These arrangements are good for increasing the capacity utilisation without incurring additional financing costs, and are certainly good in a very volatile market; though returns are somewhat lower. You may consider these arrangements once the level of production you are aiming at has been reached.

Do not get tied down to full-time job-work contracts. Never accept conversion norms tighter than you experience in your operation. Try and pass on as much fixed cost as possible under manufacturing costs. Insist on a bank guarantee. And, finally, try and smuggle in a minimum-volume clause in the agreement.

Measures for raising finances

There are several ways of raising finances and there are good chances that you have tried some of them. However, the list given below need not be a complete waste and you may find some new technique here. You must note that not all these ways are open to all the units. No method is cost-free. Each endangers something and offers some advantages.

1. Obtaining equipment under lease or hire-purchase schemes: This is quite similar to hiring the equipment. There are a few more features to lease/hire purchase schemes. These have to do with depreciation, lease rentals, down-payments and effective interest charges. For items which are depreciated at normal rates (25 per cent), the effective credit cost comes in the range of 26 to 30 per cent. There is scope to negotiate, but not too much.

How Best to Manage Your Finances

2. Unsecured privately accepted deposits: This has become quite a common method of raising finance. In fact, this way a lot of unaccounted money gets deployed for productive purposes through the intermediation of accounting and tax consultants. You may accept this money, but try and avoid offering cash interest for reasons discussed in sections on Blunders 3 and 4. Actually, giving cash interest is a luxury you can ill afford. You may like to offer an interest rate much higher than bank rates, but in white, in the formal cheque payment mode. Try something in the range of 27 per cent. Most people wanting to park their unaccounted funds will find it tempting. And, of course, it is still cheaper than giving two per cent in cash.

3. Formal debt instruments: Usually not feasible for the small industry, these include accepting unsecured public deposits, issuing commercial paper or partly convertible/non-convertible debentures. The small industrial unit is perhaps in a position to accept public deposits, but then the hassles and formalities are quite substantial.

4. Formal banking channel: This should be the most preferred mode of borrowing as this is the least expensive and most respectable. The only trouble often is that most entrepreneurs stretch their goodwill with bankers and ruin the possibility of getting credit limits enhanced. These days there has been considerable decentralisation and very substantially increased competition in commercial banking and banks are on the lookout for worthy borrowers. If your slate is clean and your financial practices have been sound, there are good chances of your requests for special, temporary credits for buying cheap materials in season being sanctioned.

5. Raising money through bought-out deals: This is one of the cheapest ways of raising equity finance. It is also very good from the point of reducing the leverage. What happens is that some merchant banker, if he is convinced of the worth of your firm and project in hand (including expansion of operations), agrees to buy a chunk of your firm's equity. He may then place it privately, or keep it with himself. He usually wants it at a discount to the fair price (e.g., for Rs 9 lakh, you will give him one lakh shares of Rs 10 each, giving a discount of 10 per cent). Such deals are possible for amounts far smaller than necessary for even an OTCEI issue, and work out much cheaper than any public issue.

The danger is that the merchant banker acquires a significant, if not dominant, stake in the firm and may be in a position to buy you out. But you need not become paranoid. Any institutional merchant banker will be unlikely to want to do such a thing. After all, there isn't exactly a queue of people who want to takeover your unit, is there?

6

Understanding and Managing Competition

The what and where of competition

Unfortunately for all businesses, competition is endemic and inevitable. It must be faced. It arises due to the working of the 'invisible hand'. In the absence of any competition for a particular product or service, the firm supplying it starts making very high profits. Since capital flows in the direction of highest profits, soon other firms start making and offering the same product or service and you have competition in that line.

According to the leading management consultant Michael Porter, competition comes from four major sources:
- Other firms existing in the industry;
- Forward integration by suppliers of raw materials to the firm/industry;
- Backward integration by buyers of the industry; and
- Makers of substitute products which can serve the same purpose.

While only the first is called industry competition, others give an overall picture of the possible competition in the medium term.

There may be a single firm offering a given product in the market or there may be several firms. The following factors determine the number of firms in a single market:
- The total size of the market;

- Minimum economic size of any firm given the technology;
- Ease of setting up the factory and business for making and selling that product; and
- Ease or difficulty of stopping the business.

For example, given the technology of the railways, only one company can run trains in a given region. Otherwise there will be expensive duplication of tracks, rolling stock and signalling systems. But there can be quite a few bread-making units in a given city.

Sometimes, it may become difficult to set up a business because it needs very large investments, too many skilled employees, the government does not give permission or the technology for making its product is protected under patents laws. Such difficulties are called *barriers to entry*.

It may be difficult to stop running the business because:

- The labour laws are very unfriendly;
- The assets and facilities are useless for any other purpose and hence too great a loss of disinvestment;
- There is a question of image and prestige of the company; or
- The owner feels that stopping the business means a great personal defeat for him.

Such difficulties for stopping the business are called *barriers to exit*.

Within the same industry there may be competition between firms who make the same or very similar product, say, the competition between different manufacturers of air-coolers in Nagpur. Such a competition is called *generic competition*. Alternatively, there may be competition between two substantially different products both of which serve the same purpose. Competition between scooters, mopeds and motor cycles is quite similar to this. Such competition may be called *competition between products*.

Generally, if the market for the product in question is increasing (i.e., if the product is in the growth phase of its life cycle), if there are significant barriers to entry but very low barriers to exit, if the firms can deploy the productive resources for making an alternate product with very little change, then the generic competition between existing firms is not intense. By contrast, if the market for the product is stagnant or shrinking, if the productive assets are very product-specific and if there are low barriers to entry but high barriers to exit, the generic competition can be very intense and bloody.

Objectives and methods of managing competition

There are two basic objectives in managing competition. The first objective is to protect and if possible increase both, the returns on investment as well as market share of your (focal) firm. The second is to create difficulty, delay and even avoid entry of likely new competitors to the industry. Firms make use of all possible and legal methods to keep existing industry competitors in check and potential competitors at bay.

Some of the common methods of doing so are developing product/brand loyalty, increasing switching costs, product differentiation, finely-tuned market segmentation and product positioning, strengthening the distribution muscle, developing cost-quality profiles, scale of operations, cornering critical supplies and resources using legal and quasi-legal instrument by manipulation etc. These concepts are explained below.

Product/service loyalty: For sometime, Doordarshan has been telecasting advertisements showing why it is more beneficial to advertise on the electronic medium rather than in the print medium. What it is trying is to create loyalty to the service offered by the medium of television. The ad could help Zee, ATN or Jain, but it will help *all* TV media as opposed to newspapers and magazines.

Most men who cherish a macho (he-man) image about themselves prefer to use motor-cycles. They would rather walk than go on a Luna. They are loyal to the product. Irrespective of brand features, products in the same class made by different competitors have a large number of common features. These features create such fierce loyalties that they can resist competition from other products which offer the same service.

Increasing switching costs: As the customer uses a particular product, he/she gets used to some patterns of behaviour, tastes, preferences and so on. The baby must adjust to momentary wetness if wrapped in a disposable diaper, the consumer of tea must get used and hooked on to the particular flavour, the rider of a motor-cycle must get used to using leg operated gears, the user of a computer must get used to a particular hardware specs, and so on.

These patterns of behaviour can be made soothing, comforting, habit forming. They become a part of the life-style of the user. This happens so completely that there are great physical or psychological difficulties if he were to use a competing product. These difficulties are called *switching costs*. A Wills smoker like me often prefers to go without a smoke rather than hold some other foul-smelling competing poison brand in my lips. The *kamwali* creates a ruckus if the powder to scrub utensils is changed. Your child refuses to eat an ice-cream not made by Dinshaws. These are examples of how switching costs can help a particular firm compete with other sellers.

Brand loyalty: When the resistance of buyers to change over to a competing brand is based on something far less material than switching costs, it is said to be pure brand loyalty. The reasons could be glamour (e.g., young women using Lux because Juhi Chawla uses it), snob value (as in the advertisement for Tata Estate), hero worship (*Kapil Dev ka*—I mean—*Palmolive ka jawab nahin*) or some such thing. The insubstantial nature of brand loyalties is often demonstrated by blind tests. For example, it has sometimes been demonstrated that smokers cannot distinguish between their so-called preferred brand and others. Brand loyalty can be developed through psychological appeals via advertisements and communications to consumers.

Market segmentation and product positioning: The two things go hand-in-hand but are different. Market segmentation means dividing the market according to some concrete parameters such as age, sex, income and education. This can, obviously, be done only if the persons in different categories behave differently in regard to the product. Product positioning is to try and create a particular image in the mind of the buyers about the product. Some marketers have a machine-gun approach: the same product in the same packaging is offered to all sorts of consumers. This is the good old Colgate model, and its early start and strong distribution helped it garner huge shares. Others carefully select a relatively smaller but choosy market segment and create product form and brand equity to cater to it. This is the Close-up model where the sex-appeal conscious adolescent and youth market is selected and pampered.

In general, the less the technical and performance basis of product assessment, greater is the gimmickry involved in market segmentation and positioning with all its allied consequences on advertisements and promotion.

Developing cost-quality profiles: The Rs 15 per kilo Hipolin and the Rs 90 a kilo Surf Ultra are both detergents. One is focused on low-price end of the market, the other on the high-price end. This gives the example of two competing products offering two sharply contrasted cost-quality profiles. The firm has to choose the specific profile it wants, keeping in mind the market size and the returns. More importantly, the rest of the operations have to be geared to exploit the chosen profile. Surf Ultra cannot be offered very effectively on credit to slum-dwellers and Hipolin cannot be sold very successfully in a supermarket in Delhi's uptown Vasant Kunj. The logistics, the advertisement, promotion and so on have to be consistent.

Cornering critical resources: The firm may tie suppliers down to long-standing binding contracts using up most of their capacity. This makes it difficult for a competitor to start. This is what soft drink sellers do by contracting for huge supplies of bottles. Hoteliers do the same in summer to *paneer* units and in winter to poultry units. Alternatively, the firm may tie up the storage, shelf space and working capital of the most logical retailer of the product. This makes it expensive and difficult for the competitor to reach his product to consumers. This is what HLL routinely does in the soaps and detergents markets.

Using legal and quasi-legal measures: Sometimes firms inform and incite the PFA officers, pollution controller, taxman and so on if the competitor is vulnerable on a relevant score. This is a dirty trick and may lead to boycott of the firm by others. But the BVO scare two years back, the clove oil suit against Promise, routine use of MRTPC, encouraged 'discovery of a dead lizard' at the bottom of a baby food tin, squealing on tax evasion by the oil trade, are all examples of some of the practices adopted to keep the competitors at bay.

Deterring entry of potential competitors

As stated earlier, competition can also come from the suppliers' forward integration in the incumbent's products, the buyers' backward integration and the maker of the substitute product for the same purpose. The last is taken first for illustration.

A decade ago the woven HDPE (high density poly-ethelene) sack offered a tremendous threat to the gunny sack-makers in India. The jute trade and industry got together and lobbied against permission for its manufacture by using every possible trick: arguments based on non-renewable energy consumption by plastics, bio-degradable, employment effect in jute mills, threat to jute production in the impoverished eastern tract, and so on.

Patriotism of the Indian seed industry has become very prominent of late strangely coinciding with the anti-Dunkel rallies and even attacks on MNC seed sellers' properties. Whether and to what extent such rallies enjoy the support of domestic seed suppliers is not known. The point is that the potential entry of a substitute product invokes a unified response from the industry as a whole as all the firms dealing with that product are affected.

At the firm level, however, more functional competitive responses are desirable. Generally the principle in competing with a potential entrant whether with a substitute product or otherwise is to make his entry unattractive, unprofitable, difficult and cumbersome. Such actions are called entry deterrents. Barriers to entry come from many potential sources: patenting a technology, raising investment levels by introducing costly product features, developing low variable cost-mass production techniques, buying up critical resources, preventing the entrant from their use, fully exploiting the learning curve, market saturation by flooding or advance supplies, contracting all major buyers and holding the contract as a legal weapon against them, using the rest of the product line as a carrot-cum-stick against deserting distributors, and selling at the entry deterring price are some of these actions.

How should you fight competition?

First, let me tell you how you should *not* fight competition. Try and avoid, to the extent possible, reduction of price as a way of fighting competition. That causes a lot of damage.

In the first place, the customer is left with a strong feeling that for all the while in the past you were charging far too much and he suddenly starts distrusting you.

Second, it is very difficult to reduce price for only one customer or even in only one place. The moment others come to know you have reduced prices in Bombay, they will either demand lower prices in Nagpur or simply delay their purchases to the extent possible. Sooner or later, the competitor will make overtures to them, or they will write to him and then you have to go to them with your tail between the legs.

Third, price reduction is a game two can play at. Virtually no entrant to any product line expects to start making money in the very first sale; he is all set to offer rich discounts, schemes such as one on one and long credit periods. When you reduce price, he will match it. In fact, he can always say, 'Irrespective of his price, I will charge three rupees less!' and then where will you stop?

The second foolish way of competing is by giving longer credit to buyers. That is a deadly game. You should allow credit only if your firm is rich with cash and bank balances, which is unlikely if you are growing. Or else you will end up committing Blunder 2 or 3.

Four sure winners in competition are: developing a niche, keeping consistent quality, earning a reputation for reliability in delivery schedules and quality, and superior after-sales customer relations and service. Most other methods (massive advertising blitzkrieg, heavy dealer discounts, and promotional schemes such as prize competitions and lotteries) can produce only short-term results and are expensive. I shall briefly explain each of these four sure winners.

Developing a niche

If you are going on a journey deep into a hilly forest, which motor-car would you take—A Standard NE, a Maruti 1000, a Padmini or a Jeep? This is the perfect example of systematically developing and exploiting a niche.

A marketing niche means a very special set of use conditions and requirements which occur in predictable circumstances. Bumpy roads, mud tracks, steep climbs, the need to cross rivulets and *nallahs*—such is the set of likely conditions in a hilly and forested area. The Jeep is designed specifically to suit such conditions and negotiate such a landscape. It is therefore not surprising that the Jeep is, in fact, used virtually by every one in this situation.

Is it possible for you to think about a niche in the product market of your business? The identification of such a niche needs a thorough understanding of the market and also a very competent design of the product and the service for the purpose. Once defined, the niche marketer is at a great advantage over all the competitors. Where he offers something uniquely right for the situation, other products need a lot of modifications. He is, naturally, preferred. The counter-point to niche marketing is that a niche marketer has a relatively limited market—no one buys a Jeep for going to shop with his wife and children. He could thus face the danger of over-specialisation. On the other hand, the advantages are much higher per unit margins and assured sales.

Maintaining consistent quality

Have you seen a Crompton ceiling fan *not* working? I have used fans for 30 years and seen many other fans breaking down, but I have not come across a Crompton fan which has broken down. It is perhaps the most consistent performer in India's manufactured products. Is it surprising that Crompton fans have enjoyed very high market shares and price leadership for four decades? Doing this obviously takes a lot of effort. Patient evolution of the production process, rigorous quality control of raw materials and at intermediate stages, ruthless rejection of substandard products, willingness to pay for high-value expensive components, etc., are needed for earning such a reputation. This is one of the surest guarantees of long-term success in the market.

It is important to produce goods of the highest possible quality for a given price (that is, given the chosen cost-quality profile). It is at times counter-productive to insist on a standard of quality which the market neither accepts nor wants. Otherwise one ends up with a marketing fiasco. See Box 6.1 for examples of such fiasco.

BOX 6.1
The story of the mouse-trap

Tens of millions were spent on creating a fabulous institute for training young boys and girls for management positions in organisations which were hopelessly undermanaged. People came from far and wide and admired the Institute and its excellent facilities. Students soon learnt that it offered very high-brow education and made a beeline for it. The clients however were unmoved. They essentially wanted their 'sons of soil' to be so trained that they would remain obsequiously obedient with some smattering of management so that the rulers of these client organisations as well as their existing rustic staff would not feel threatened. Also, such rustic MBAs would come quite cheap. The nine-day wonder graduates of this Institute expected a lot from these organisations, seldom got it and soon moved to greener pastures. Thus, despite doing a very fine job of training smart and bright MBAs, the Institute was always told that it did not do its job well. The MBAs were unwanted by those for whom they were trained.

The moral of the story is: you cannot make a chrome-steel mouse-trap and expect to sell it easily to those who just want to kill rats and could as well do with rat poison!

This is not the only example of producing goods of a quality far better than what the market desires and is willing to pay for. A famous chocolate manufacturer of the country went on remorselessly making chocolates according to international

> specifications. (The chocolate, it seems, should melt on its own when put in the international mouth.) That meant making a chocolate with low melting point. That would have been fine in any country where the ambient temperatures were also low. In India, you seldom wanted to buy that brand because the gooey muck made to international standards would stick to the wrapping paper! The manufacturer was finally saved by the popularisation of cold chains in the distribution network.

Naturally, quality is only for a price, and comparison of one's product should be made with the products which offer the same cost-quality profile. It is also very important to be consistent. A product of good quality should not be a matter of accident but design. Maintaining consistent quality is where many small enterprises lack. As was mentioned earlier, the coming years of intense competition will see the survival of only those manufacturers who provide products of good and consistent quality.

Reliability

Reliability is a technical word, the precise meaning of which is an amplification of its simple English meaning. High reliability means essentially very low probability of non-performance. Clearly, reliability of the firm includes the quality of its product but also includes many other things as well.

Consider the case of a firm selling pouched milk to its consumers. Assume that the consumers are told that the milk will contain 3.1 per cent fat and 9 per cent SNF, each pouch will have 500 ml milk, that it will be delivered between 7 am and 8 am, and will remain good without boiling or refrigeration till noon.

High reliability means that in a whole year or such long periods, there is virtually no variation in *any* one of the four performance parameters. The reputation for reliability is invariably built *over time*, when the firm is seen to deliver high quality performance again and again. That is a very demanding thing to achieve, but once achieved, stands in good stead to the firm. To achieve high reliability, the internal systems have to be built well, many back-ups have to be created and the firm's managers have to exercise ceaseless vigil over the functioning units.

Superior after-sales service and support

Many insurance agents chase you till you get tired of them. They stick to you as close as your shadow when you indicate interest in buying a policy. Once you have completed formalities and bought the policy, they rarely show their faces to you again.

This is the case of no after-sales service. Usually, you tend to have very bitter feelings about these agents and try to go to some one else next time. Does your firm behave like an insurance agent with its customers? Or does it offer after-sales support and service?

Sometimes firms offer after-sales service contracts for capital goods and machinery, and not very unusually the customers run away from them even faster because of the kind of contract and the kind of service given under it.

I will confine myself to talking about simple maintenance of good relations and contacts with the customer. Surely, when you sell the material to him, you have his telephone number. It is a good idea to keep in touch with the customer at a personal level. Many of you keep contact in a very distant and impersonal form by sending printed greeting cards. Does it cost too much to give a ring once in a while and ask how he feels about the material or the machine sent?

You will say that when you ring up customers like this, they only complain, and that tells me how infrequently you do it. If on hearing the complaint for the first time, you make genuine attempts to satisfy the customer (always assuming you have sold him something of a reasonable quality and not a lemon), next time he will be very courteous. And repeating these inexpensive acts helps you keep tab of market developments, gauge when the next stage of demand and hence order is coming and earn for yourself the name of a fellow who can be trusted.

7
A Matter of Style

When it comes to decisions regarding the general approach to facing competition and dealing with business associates, competitors, suppliers, buyers, financiers, etc., different small-industry owners behave differently. A great deal of such behaviour is perhaps a function of the essential self-perception of the entrepreneur himself. I have observed three basic patterns which I shall describe in this chapter.

The animal kingdom has always fascinated me. Due to a certain commonality of traits between the behavioural patterns of small-industry owners and animals, I have called these the patterns of the lizard, fox and lion.

Unfortunately, to the common man, this nomenclature may evoke evaluative reactions. This is not my intention at all. It is certainly not my place to come down on any one of the approaches. In fact, there is no need. Which approach one adopts is basically a matter of style.

I shall, of course, hold forth on the implications of each of these approaches for operational decision-making. Perhaps more in keeping with my theme in the book, I shall speculate about which of the blunders come more naturally to which approach.

The current industrial atmosphere exhibits a great deal of flux. Small companies are growing big. Many big ones are getting absorbed in even bigger ones. Some are splitting. Some others are just waiting for Godot. Like many other issues discussed earlier, the three approaches I discuss below are not unique to the small industry alone. Similar patterns are shown by many larger undertakings as well.

The pattern of the lizard

What image does the word lizard conjure up for you?

To many people, the lizard represents the ultimate in creeping, slithery and repulsive ugliness. I admit that no lizard will ever win a beauty contest. But one must look at the other side. To me, the very mention of the word lizard symbolises the essence of the art of survival. The lizard, like the mongoose and the tortoise, is among the oldest surviving species.

I know of no house which is devoid of lizards, and yet they are never obvious. Only after you have spent sometime in a strange house, and are vacantly focusing on the wall or the ceiling, do you suddenly notice the lizard. It is invariably silent. You do not like it and may chase it with a broom. It never waits to growl and threaten you but very meekly runs away behind a wall hanging or a cupboard. You feel glad and victorious and as you gloat over your grand victory, it has already emerged from its hiding to chase another moth or insect on the opposite side of the wall.

Among all the people who have chased lizards, few have caught it by surprise: the creepy creature is always alert. Once the lizard has spotted its prey, just watch it plan its moves. Slowly and imperceptibly but with a determined design it approaches the hapless prey. Then with lightning speed it pounces upon it to gobble it up leaving you wondering how could it manage to swallow such a large insect?

And except when another lizard teases it or some thing, it seems not to mind its competitors at all. During the rainy season you can watch five—may be six—lizards on the same wall busily gobbling up those wretched winged ants and other insects. (By now I am sure you feel that consultants do nothing but vacantly watch walls for the movement of lizards!)

When I write that some entrepreneurs adopt the strategic style of the lizard, what does the parable signify to you? The lizard's management pattern is like the unassuming, self-effacing, low key, unostentatious, persevering entrepreneur who intends, at all costs, to survive.

This type of entrepreneur has no use for the pomp and splendour of a modern office. No polished doors and smiling receptionists, perhaps no computers, possibly there may even be a leaky roof and—believe me, I have seen this—an ink-stained and soiled table-cloth on the MD's table.

He does not waste money on full-page newspaper advertisements; his products are plastered in ugly profusion over walls along the railway line. Nor will he give his dealers a dinner in five-star hotels. Rather, he feeds them sumptuous home food in his own home in the company of his wailing grandchildren. He lives in a well-knit network of other businessmen-lizards. These are the fellows who are content to have their plates full of business from second-grade clients, who believe in the perpetual existence of the lower-middle class and mean to make money catering to its simple needs. And they survive for generations.

This type of an entrepreneur is apt to make Blunders 4, 5 and 7. He belongs to the genre in which the number of bankruptcies measures business astuteness and will hence try to be smart in a slithery way. Informal, zero-tax dealings are the norm rather than the exception. Floating a number of firms to avoid tax is an act of the same basic pettifogging nature. And because their firms are so lacking in glamour, hardly anybody outside the lizard clan except the down-and-outers will join them. So they make a virtue out of necessity by hiring cheap Harirams.

I must emphasise that there is nothing inherently problematic with this strategic style of management. One must, of course, realise its implications. They are as follows:

- There is a deliberate emphasis on informality. Trust and loyalty of the cheap Harirams, either those from the lizard family itself or the down-and-outers, are far more important to the entrepreneurs than their competence.
- The entrepreneur keeps weaving webs of deception at such a pace that no one except himself and his *munim* or some other very trusted lieutenant can unravel all the mysteries of his accounting universe. He himself is not really beyond the ordinary pitfalls faced by mortals:

accidents, sickness, acute family traumas and so on, and premature death. And in those events, the whole enterprise receives a major, sometimes irreparable, setback. Of course, one has also heard countless stories of the trusted *munim* deciding that his need for the coin is larger than that of the *seth*.
- The business can really deal with only low technology grimy, unpleasant and filthy things: commodities processing in general, dealing with hazardous chemicals and so on. And naturally for such business lines, anonymity helps. High or even medium-technology businesses will need people who will find it suffocating to work in the lizard's hole and creep on its rather restricted walls. Hence, the entrepreneur is faced with limited choice even when he wants to become large and grow along more interesting lines.

But for survival in the existing line, the lizard is perhaps the most optimally suited. His low-key style means very little overheads; he has far greater flexibility and far less ego problems. He is very swift in making decisions and swifter still in implementing his commercial decisions. In fact, he is the backbone of Indian small industry.

The pattern of the lion

I have really not watched too many lions in real life. One meets so few of them socially these days. Therefore, I have had to rely on second-hand information and judgements of what a lion is and should be like. These are popular perceptions and are reinforced by Disney and other purveyors of stereotypes. People have a way of lionising so many scoundrels and pigs these days; there can certainly be little harm in lionising a lion.

Since I am primarily dealing with small industries, the more appropriate allegory would be that of the lion cub. But I shall continue to call this the pattern of the LION for the sake of contrast with the lizard. In fact, the very title suggests that the contrast is nearly complete. The lizard is low-key, unobtrusive, willing to go into a hiding when threatened and so on.

The lion is nothing of the kind. He is bold, brave and daring. He does not yield to threats meekly, but will growl, fight, attack and pounce. He believes that he is born to lead and to rule. He is confident that he has the ability to win. He is raring to establish and expand his empire. He has an almost inextinguishable pride in possession of his territory.

There is a lot of glamour about a lion and he loves being idolised. If at all he acknowledges the lizards' existence, he looks at them with disdain. Perhaps he is too preoccupied with his own majesty and tends to err on the side of imprudence, taking rather wild risks for the sake of protecting the dignity and pride of the lions.

The lions, among small-scale entrepreneurs, either remain small or become leading industrialists in a very short time. They are either soon acknowledged as shining examples of pioneering industrial leadership or thrown in the junk heap of the industrial backyard, forgotten by all.

Lions are live-wire, high-profile, devil-may-care go-getters who are willing to take chances. They are never content to cater, like the lizard, to the second grade and the lower-middle class. They like acclaim, appreciation and accolades. They are ever willing to proclaim their presence. The full-page advertisements and five-star dinners are definitely their actual or desired way of life.

They are certainly not scared of the competition but will growl and pounce menacingly when threatened. Very possessive of their market shares and geographical areas, they give the competition a run for its money. In their organisation, they like being surrounded by people and things which add to their pioneering leadership image. You will find the lions to be the first among their peers to acquire new toys and gadgets (like the E-mail and the pagers or advanced equipment for automatic manufacture or R & D labs).

They gather talented people around them and retain them by dint of sheer personal magnetism. Their talented subordinates may actually hero worship them and stay with them because they obtain a vicarious sense of fulfilment from the successes of the boss. And because they gather good people, they can install modern and progressive practices.

Then where is the catch? Well, the lion-hero may soon turn out to have feet of clay. He may be seen to become petty, squeamish, scared or even incapable of translating his grandiose plans into action. Then, the talented subordinates leave him faster than they joined him.

In our country talented young men are a dime a dozen and this is therefore not a disaster. But what is really tragic is that the lion is always in a hurry to grow. He takes risks. He is thus prone to make Blunders 2 and 3. So completely assured is he of his own tell-a-tale skills of prediction and astute business acumen, that he soon abandons elementary caution.

Potential gains in the form of extra turnover and profits cast a magic spell over him and he tends to forget that leverage is a two-edged sword. The subordinates are too mesmerised by his charismatic sway to tell him that he is taking a foolhardy risk. The firm is very likely to be ruined by his tendency to take undue financial risks for speculative business moves. He bites more than he can chew. The rest soon becomes history.

Alternatively he may play around with some laws in what he thinks is true buccaneer fashion and even proclaim having done so, only to find his loud-mouthed bragging bringing his ruin. Most lions are mature enough to be more discreet. But the trouble is that the dividing line between the lion and the buccaneer is thin, almost imperceptible and any day the lion may overstep.

But we all like the lion cubs who grow and rule the industrial jungles. The Ambanis who emerged virtually from nowhere to become the most awesome name in Indian industry are the role models for many an industrialist. A few heroes of the lion mould are the Mehtas of Torrent group, the Handas of Core group, Sanghvi of the Sun, Rajratnam the new-breed raider among others.

The pattern of the fox

The image of the fox is that of a scheming, shrewd, almost wicked creature. He certainly wants the good things of life. But he doesn't want to fight for them as he lacks the required physical prowess, nor does he wish to work for them. He is invariably seen to rely on his manipulative skills in arranging for situations to become favourable to him. By doing so, he averts the need for a fight and the work is done by others.

The popular image of the fox, based on the Aesop fables and countless other folklores, is one of a cunning and wicked creature. But when you look at it dispassionately, why should the fox be considered wicked? He is interested in his well being and looks out for himself. Is that a crime? Should one rather be cunning or naive? I, for one, would not mind becoming a member of the Saintly Fox Society, if there is such a thing. I consider the fox to be a good fellow, so those of my readers who fall in the fox pattern need not become angry.

The sociologist, V. Pareto (the same scholar who gave the elusive concept of Pareto Optimality), has suggested on allegory of the fox in opposition to that of the lion. To him, lion is the brave and bold warrior who wins the world around him by might and valour. The fox, on the other hand, is believed to rely more on brain than brawn. The fox, therefore, cherishes knowledge, foresight, analysis and other such cerebral activities. The lions, generally, are said be direct, open and confident without being too analytical. The foxes are subtle, circumspect, inclined to adapt indirect and often underhand methods. This is the sense in which the pattern of the fox is to be understood.

The management pattern of the fox is that of employing vile and guile to try and reach its competitive objective without too much commitment of resources. Principally, if the fight is not winnable, the fox does not start it. He believes in the philosophy 'If you cannot beat them, join them'. The entrepreneur who comes to believe that he doesn't stand a chance of winning a competitive battle against an MNC giant, then starts manufacturing for the MNC on job-work basis fits this pattern.

The fox certainly means to thrive and grow, but not by open warfare. Its industrial equivalence is doing contract manufacture, selling on consignment basis, getting involved in an ancillary relationship, accepting controls on quality and production methods, even getting taken over.

The fox's principal strategy is to conserve energies and resources by biding for an opportue time when its own resources are strong enough to stake a bold and brave lion-like claim. The fox may adopt some interesting stances, such as expensive public-relation exercises on some occasions combined with extreme resource conservation in general. He is not seen to be over committing, nor is he pettifogging; he believes in slowly, systematically gathering strength.

The fox almost never gets caught in Blunders 2 and 3. Since he is more keen to progressively grow from strength to strength, he often concentrates on production and logistics on the buying side, leaving the marketing to the consignment agent or the principal buyer. His most likely pitfall, therefore, is Blunder 1, i.e., overdependence on one buyer.

So why should you worry about it?

At the beginning of this chapter I had said that decisions are matters of style and need not be evaluated in the sense of being good or bad. Looked at another way, the three patterns described above are also expressions of implied strategy.

The pattern of the lizard essentially symbolises the strategy of an entrepreneur who knows he is a small man and does not therefore harbour grandiose dreams. He wishes to remain small and trim, providing services necessary for the chosen client in a low key but fairly dependable manner. Price and personal service rather than high-fidelity performance of products are his selling points. His marketing style is low key, relying perhaps on trade discounts of all sorts rather than high pressure advertising and promotion, building personal relationships with dealers and other elements of the chain. Long-term survival—principally by being anonymous, unobtrusive and unnoticeable—lies at the core of the lizard's strategy.

The fox's approach is to avoid all non-winnable fights, aiming for growth by joining forces with potential allies, converting threatening situations into nurturing ones through negotiations, etc. The fox is less committed to a very sharp definition of product-market profile than to his long-term growth. In its most comprehensive sense, strategy is truly employed by the fox.

The lion's approach is one of staking a claim and defending it vigorously. His strategy is actually very explicit on goals but less so on means. It is usually even naively optimistic on the resource-mobilisation front.

Ultimately, it is up to the entrepreneur to choose among the three strategies while deciding how his enterprise should evolve in the changing environment. He has to first recognise which pattern most closely resembles his current style of operation. Then he has to figure out whether the likely implications of the pattern are to his liking and how he must set about changing the strategic style of his business. For, strategic choices in relation to competition will force consistency throughout the enterprise and the entrepreneur may, on his own accord, move towards it.

8

Managing the Pangs of Growth

Growth in sales turnover, gross profit, PAT and cash inflows is a very happy thing to happen. All industrialists dream about it. I have not come across a single industrialist whose five-year projections show constancy or negative trend in any one of these parameters. And as I have argued earlier, in the new economic environment, growth is no more a matter of choice; it is a categorical imperative.

Each small industry must grow bigger and bigger, if for no other reason than merely to survive. The environment around the small industry is such that it has to run faster merely to keep being in the same place. However necessary and pleasant the end result of growth may be, it is by no means an easy process. There are fairly severe growth pains. In this chapter, I shall deal with ways of mitigating growth pains and offer suggestions about what may prove to be the best options.

Four important issues are involved in the process of growth. They are: matching asset expansion with sales growth, managing finances, systematically expanding sales and maintaining and improving quality. The first and the second are interrelated. First of all, sales growth almost always occurs incrementally and smoothly, say 3 per cent more each month with seasonal dips, etc. While it becomes clear to the entrepreneur that his existing human and material facilities are running out of their capacity, the choice of addition of capacity is problematic.

Fresh capacity cannot always be created in small increments. You cannot add 3 per cent extra capacity per month with seasonal dips, except when you are making completely labour-dependent products. At this stage the tendency is also to acquire specialised rather than general-purpose machinery and the match of their capacities *entre se* is always difficult and problematic. Each individual piece of machinery has its own economically optimal capacity. (For example, while you need only 300 kg steam per hour now, conceivably you need more next year but you are not sure. The man in charge of the boiler tells you that the most efficient boilers are in the two MT range, and you don't know what to make of it.) That is why matching of asset expansion with sales turnover is an important facet of managing growth.

Associated with this is the second and the most crucial element of growth, namely management of finances. Cash input per unit of turnover is nearly always the highest at the growth phase, and hence you need a lot of working capital. You therefore find that while you are doing more and more business, there is never any cash and you are all the time trying to postpone payments of all sorts. Then, asset expansion also needs a lot of lumpy capital. At this stage one is most prone to misjudge the potential leverage bearing capacity, something on which I have focused at some length in Chapter 5. The relevant financial management concepts are merely touched upon here.

The third factor related to growth is systematic and planned growth of sales and the techniques for introducing that spirit in the firm rather than leaving growth to chance or to the environment. Planning for marketing effort is something which is seldom done but those who do so obtain very rewarding results.

The fourth important matter pertains to improvement of quality. It is believed quite falsely that improvement of quality can only be possible by basically increasing the cost of the product. Since a lot of small industry—of the lizard type, at any rate—is catering to the extremely price sensitive lower-middle class market, the industry is unwilling to even think in terms of quality improvement. Their customer gets a good quality product purely by great good luck. That there is an urgent need to change this approach of 'quality by chance' to 'quality by design' there can be no doubt. But that substantial upgradation is possible even without necessarily increasing product cost is ill understood. I shall expand on this.

Matching asset expansion with sales growth

When sales start growing steadily month after month, at some point in time the production capacity becomes inadequate. The production process may involve, say, five stages or sub-processes (including intermediate storages). Not all of them become crowded at once. The 'bottle-neck' process starts getting jammed. This sets the entrepreneur thinking about expansion. But he is prudent. He knows that he should be patient and not expand the assets unless things have stabilised in the old facilities and he has acquired full control on his markets. Acquisition, installation and utilisation of new asset is problematic and need full-time application on the part of the entrepreneur. To use a military phrase, he should not open a second front if he is unsure of the first.

The entrepreneur does what he can to make maximum use of the facilities: using the remaining shifts, minor modifications to enhance capacity, getting work done on a contract basis, etc. Yet things start becoming difficult. It is then that the problem becomes acute.

Often the problem of production bottle-necks is of a seasonal nature. In a certain season, the capacity falls short of the required production. For example, the notebook manufacturer finds that the facilities for paper cutting and binding are inadequate during June. This is because he has to cater to the demand at the time of opening of schools. The manufacturer of air-coolers finds that there is insufficient capacity to manufacture coolers during March-April which is his peak season. And so on.

In the rest of the year, there is enough capacity as there is hardly any sale. So the first-hand solution is to start making for the peak season a month or two earlier. That needs storage space as well as working capital. So one finds that the notebook-maker's factory, godown, shop, home even courtyard become chock-a-block with notebooks. Or the cooler-maker's factory has so many coolers that he has to ask you to sit on one of them while you chat. But this can be risky as the seasonal working capital need has to be usually managed through informally borrowed funds. That brings us back to Blunder 3. The hazards of fire faced by the notebook-maker is a separate category of risk, and each product has its special kind of risk of destruction. So the choice really is either facing annual risk of keeping large stocks of saleable goods a couple of months ahead of season or to enhance capacity.

Four basic options to the problem of matching asset expansion to sales growth exist. They are:

- Seasonal or temporary leasing of facilities wherever available;
- Duplication of existing facilities;
- Incremental addition to facilities as each bottle-neck is expanded and the next becomes constraining; and
- Acquisition of a brand new, next-generation package of processing facilities for a higher capacity.

The choice among them is dependent on the degree of commitment you have to the product line, your financial muscle and perception of the pattern of growth.

If the growth is purely transitory, which will just boil away after a couple of months, the best option is to get temporary lease on facilities. Alternatively, one may try relieving the most crowded facility by getting the concerned operations done on job work. If the increase in sales level persists, one may think of expanding the facility. The hiring or leasing of facilities or getting critical operations on job work from outside permit much greater flexibility and time for the entrepreneur to assess the permanence of demand and hence enable him to take a more balanced decision on capacity expansion.

To ensure that the products that are sold under the same trade name have uniform quality, it is important to ensure that those made from the old facilities as well as those from the new are similar to each other. Second, growth is sufficiently engaging and entrepreneurs should not complicate the matter by introducing unfamiliar technology. With these things in mind, a lot of entrepreneurs favour just plain duplication of existing facilities in the same premises if they can help, or in other premises if they have to.

This is like a potter installing the second wheel and clearing up another part of the courtyard for sun-drying his earthenware and adding another wood-fired open hearth for baking them. No qualitative change at all. He may even 'duplicate' himself by asking his son to sit at the second wheel!

This method offers the major advantage that entrepreneurs do not have to learn anything new. They know the basic control parameters of the process and hence feel comfortable with the new facilities. The disadvantage is that the entrepreneur does not make any qualitative or technological improvement in the product.

When the perception of growth encourages permanent expansion of facilities of somewhat better technological features but own resource are insufficient and the entrepreneur does not wish to take too much risk of debt (the most prevalent situation in the industry), incremental addition of facilities is done. The machine or the process which causes the most severe bottle-neck is expanded first, then the next and so on till in about five years, this cycle is ready to repeat all over again. In case of a phased manner of expansion, blueprint of facilities to be acquired eventually should be made.

If this is not done, several problems may occur. In the first place, the question of capacity. If the extra demand is only 500 on an existing level of sales of 1,000 units, you really need a facility capable of producing at the most 1,000 units. But when you scout around for equipment you discover that the minimum economic size of the machines of the company you would like to buy from has already crossed 2,500. That will mean very substantial slack even if you sell off the old plant, for which there may be no market any way. Now what do you do?

Entrepreneurs tend to shop around for small-capacity plants and somewhere someone is always making a smaller version of everything. Are the options of job work or wet lease inferior to buying some unknown make just because you get it in the small size.

As you keep adding machines, the problem of incompatibility between machines starts coming up. High tech machines tend to be demanding and perfectionist in regard to intermediate stages as well, and if the existing machinery is the backyard type, just one high tech machine somewhere along the line will not substantially improve quality.

In the event of incremental addition of capacity, the problem of balancing the lines is inevitably forced. One way of getting around this problem is to *take* job work for the machine on which there is a slack, particularly if it is not going to interfere with your production. This way you may reduce the burden of overheads a bit.

In fact, what tends to happen in the case of unbalanced lines is that such extra work tends to be undertaken as will occupy the slack. That work becomes rewarding, tying up the facility but demanding capacity on some other machine, creating bottle-neck there and so on.

Consider, for example, the transformer wire industry. The entrepreneur finds that the wire-drawing machine is now inadequate and so acquires another. The new machine has a better performance and suddenly shoots up capacity, hence the entrepreneur introduces aluminium wires as his product in addition to copper, and now discovers that coating lines are getting choked!

The best option, particularly if you are committed to the product line and the resources can be generated by a variety of ways is to set up a completely new, higher technology and quality line. To begin with, you may run both and gradually start phasing out the first. Some entrepreneurs introduce a premium brand, run it on new lines and keep operating the old factory for the old brand as well. Such cannibalism actually expands your *total* market.

Whatever you do in this regard has to correspond with your steps in market expansion and financing arrangements. The cautionary steps to take while deciding the latter have been given in the discussion on leverage principle.

Financing asset expansion

This subject has been discussed in Blunder 1 as well as in the chapter on managing finances. Here I shall give it very brief attention, suggesting that the reader may refer to earlier sections for details.

The expansion of assets should not be financed at all unless the firm has acquired enough working capital. Thus, the first application of operating surplus is in building up working capital. Second, it is useful to keep in mind that while the financial commitment for new assets is irrevocable and lumpy, the capacity to repay the inevitable debt burden is acquired only slowly as the growth in sales sustains itself. There are also the uncertainties and seasonalities involved. Thus, the expanded asset base is bound to mean a little heavy burden of capital servicing on the existing revenues.

Hence, to the extent possible, the debt-servicing burden should be negotiated in such a manner that the cash outflow matches the generation of sales. More importantly, the entrepreneur may like to limit his risks by going in for options such as hiring capacity on other firms and hire purchase, particularly if he is unsure of the sales growth. Finally, he may like to match the asset expansion with simultaneous expansion of the equity base. This is what most entrepreneurs do. If the past record of the enterprise is not brilliant and if the existing sales and asset size is small, the entrepreneur may have to opt for things like bought-out deals. Expansion by using unsecured deposits or by taking cash loans is not recommended.

Planning for growth in sales

Growth in sales is always desirable. It is a sure sign of the firm's health. Two factors may lead to growth in value of sales.

Inflation and demographic changes, in any event, mean growth in rupee value of sales for the whole industry and hence the firm—irrespective of whether the firm makes special efforts or not. The entrepreneur should not rest content with it. True growth, of which one should be proud, occurs because the product one is making is catching people's fancy and is becoming popular, or because in an existing product one is gaining market share at the expense of the competitor.

But growth is neither certain nor a steady phenomenon. In fact it is tricky. There may be occasions during which remarkable opportunities occur, and if they are missed, then all may be lost. In most of the products and lines today, qualitatively different competition is fast emerging.

Most of the producers of Fast Moving Consumer Goods (FMCG) are putting up bigger and better facilities, and in quite a few lines there is at the moment a sort of lull before the competitive storm that looms ahead. Many small-industry entrepreneurs may be able to exploit the lull and achieve good growth if they move rapidly, that is, in about a couple of years. The advantage is an already entrenched seller is difficult to dislodge as even the giant Pepsi discovered while facing Parle. Hence, there is a need for very rapid growth in the next couple of years. Thereafter it will be the market share defence game, with the total market growing with demographic changes.

Growth may also occur through different routes, which may have a bearing on the way the production process and market logistics are organised. Growth may come from hitherto untapped rural areas, which may mean changes in product attributes, packaging and distribution logistics. Or growth may occur through popular adoption of the product for end uses not so far envisaged, but which catch up after someone is the first to do it. In any event many entrepreneurs may have to worry about planning for growth rather than growth just happening to them.

Two of the simplest causes of sales growth are *intensification* or *saturation* in an existing sales territory and *geographical expansion*. In the first, the firm increases its reach to consumers by approaching and encouraging more retailers and different kinds of retailers in selling their product. For example, the half-medicine, half-fun tablets like Halls and Vicks have increased their sales through intensification. Some years ago, Vicks drops were available only with medical shops; now they are available in provision stores, grocers, restaurants and even *paan* shops. Many parents give their children Vicks instead of mints or toffees.

The geographic expansion case is straightforward: till now you were selling only in Rajasthan, now you appoint a C&F agent in Indore and start selling in Malwa, then the whole of M.P., then Vidarbha, and so on. Let us use these two methods of growth to illustrate planning for growth rather than growth just happening to you.

Appointing distributors

Assume, for the purpose of illustration, that you are engaged in selling some FMCG (say a new pickle) and that the households are the basic buyers. Instead of looking at sales as a mere disposal-of-production problem, try looking at it as a way of building and cementing your ties with the distribution network. Think through as shown in the illustration in Box 8.1.

BOX 8.1
Thought process before appointing distributors

To sell my pickle on a regular and sustained basis, I must have a strong retail network. That will have to be regularly serviced in at least three ways:

- Supplies of new lots must be made and old unsold stock must be picked up at regular intervals;
- Regular complaint and grievance handling mechanism, perhaps combined with order booking and collections, will have to be put in place; and
- Advertisement and promotional support will have to be provided.

I know that all three are needed for a balanced and sustained sales growth. The first needs a regular wholesaler or distributor arrangement. The second needs a planned schedule of visits from salesmen and area sales managers to retailers and wholesalers. And the third needs a series of sales promotion measures to be released one after another. Let us look at the way to think through each of these three.

When will someone of repute and standing agree to be my distributor? When I can guarantee him enough business, when he sees that my product is in some way complementary to his existing lines, when he feels that my quality is good and when he feels that I am trustworthy and good. (Contrary to what you may think, virtually no distributor is looking for big profit from a new agency in the first year. He is looking at a way of further spreading his overheads and also and perhaps mainly at the products' potential.)

If I approach a distributor at a stage when a fourth of my pickle packs leak and leave oily stains, I am unable to commit a minimum supply per month to his territory and there are severe quality problems, the distributors will either shy away from me

> or drop me at the first opportunity.
> What would I like in a distributor? He should have contacts with retailers who sell allied products for households, who have infrastructure and a good name and should be financially sound. He should commit to a certain schedule of supply to his retailers. He should help me liaise with his set of clientele as well as other organisations and to assist me in developing the market.
> For ensuring that I must choose someone with whom I have a decent chance of a long-term association, I will have to spend time gathering information about potential distributors and cultivating good parties before making a choice. The sales growth can never be sustained if association with distributors is half-hearted.

The volume of sales that can be expected from any territory needs to be carefully assessed before entering it. There are several ways of doing this: analysis of secondary data, judgement of the distributors and retailers selling existing pickles and similar products, formal market surveys, etc.

One of the most promising method is to base the judgement on how many units (say packets of 500 gm) of your pickle can one retailer sell in a month. You must recognise that unless he feels that he can sell a certain minimum number of units of your product, he will not stock it at all. This is because he is under severe shelf-space constraint.

For your pickle to be visible, the retailer should display it in a proper place and also occasionally bring to the customer's notice. ('*Saheb*, try this pickle, it is very good and it is a new item!' don't you hear this many times?) But so many other products in the FMCG category require him to do the same. He will not touch your product or will not feel enthused to push it unless he feels that it has a good potential *and* unless you promise him a handsome margin (for a new product, usually upwards of 7 per cent, with promise of accepting back spoilage and unsold units, or at least 15 per cent otherwise). Even a retailer will not want to hear loud complaints and recriminations from his good customers for your bad product. So he makes a careful assessment and tells you how many he can sell.

To make a judgement of the likely volume, divide the retailers in the new territory in three categories: large, medium and small. Estimate the number of retailers in each category in your territory. Obtain an estimate from a few retailers in each of them about the quantity they can sell.

For example, suppose the Bangalore distributor has with him some 50 large retailers, 250 medium retailers and about 1,000 small retailers. Large retailers feel that they can sell some 20 packets of your pickles each month, medium fellows say they can sell at the most 10 and the small one feel at the most three. Your total volume through this distributor per month in Bangalore is 20 × 50 + 250 × 10 + 1,000 × 3 = 6,500 packs per month.

Now, if you are pricing your pickle at Rs 30 per pack and giving the distributor a 4 per cent margin, the distributor expects to make Rs 7,800 from your product. He may be enthused to push the product. The retailers whom you are giving say 8 per cent may or may not be similarly enthused (e.g., the small retailer just expects to make Rs seven each month and may not want to stock your product at all). In that case you will have to work on them, offer some scheme, etc.

Sales force

Irrespective of the quality of the distributors appointed, the firm has to appoint a sales force. The sales force like the salesmen, sales supervisors and officers perform some very important functions.

In the first place, they maintain an active and live contact with the distribution chain. The retailer or the distributor does not feel that he is being neglected. The current system of selling FMCG in India has come to place quite a substantial reliance on the repeated visits of the sales force to the field. If a small company like yours does not do it, the retailers will think that you are not a good, careful company.

Only a part of the reason for hiring the sales force is just to satisfy this expectation of the retailer that someone from the company will call on him and talk to him about the product, the market and what he feels. The second function the sales force performs is to keep giving a continuous feedback to the company about how its product is moving vis-a-vis those of the competitors, what are the typical complaints, what are the plus-points and so on.

The third function they perform is of complaint handling and solution. For this purpose, the salesmen have to be given very clear and reasonably good authority to take spot decisions (to replace spoilt packs, leaky pouches and so on). It is no use having salesmen who keep telling the retailer that they will get back to him after talking to the boss.

The fourth function the sales force performs is to chase and follow-up on collections of payments. This becomes very crucial if you yourself have been giving credit. In any event, it is good to even assist the distributor in recoveries.

The fifth function the sales force performs is to do the necessary logistical follow-up and problem solving (e.g., getting past octroi, managing sales tax formalities, solving some local delivery problem, arranging meetings for you when you visit and so on.)

The sixth function is to ensure that the POP material sent is actually used and that the retailers are displaying your product. And all these functions are, of course, in addition to the basic function of pushing up your sales by doing the salesmanship.

The sales force has to be very carefully trained in the precise nature of its seven functions listed above. They have to be made to prepare a daily schedule of visits to the retailers in their beat. The usual system of making them send daily reports helps you keep a check on them as well as ensure that these functions are, in fact, performed. And for helping them to move around, you have to pay them conveyance charges, lunch expenses and so on.

All this is an integral part of sales growth. The number of retailers a salesman visits in a day depends on how close they are located to each other, how much time you expect him to spend with the retailers and what is the load of administrative and other work on him. A lot of companies follow the system of the salesman booking orders and nursing retailers independent of the distributor's delivery movement while some others combine the two. Between 20 and 30 visits a day is a reasonable load.

You must target to have the salesman calling on each one of your retailers once a month and depending on how many retailers you have in a city, the number of salesmen needed can be decided. In the above example of Bangalore, the total number of retailers is 1,275 and hence three salesmen are required, if each is going to be visiting 25 retailers a day, spending 15 days on visits, thus allowing time for other kind of work.

Advertising and promotion

Several things are included under this head of activities. In the first place, your consumers must be at least aware that your product exists and is now available to them in their city. This calls for measures of increasing awareness about your product.

Second, there must be some efforts to make them try your product and having tried, to keep using it. Then, there have got to be incentives for the retailers for selling (usually called 'schemes' in the FMCG sales circuit).

There are also things like special campaigns for promoting the product (e.g., Camlin holds drawing competitions for children all over the country every once in a while). Finally, the retailer always feels greatly supported if you give him posters and danglers for his shop announcing your products as a Point of Purchase (hence POP) publicity material.

Advertising can use cheap media like roadside hoarding and pamphlets distributed by newspaper boys or can be as expensive as TV advertisements. The choice of medium has got to match with the progress in geographic spread of your selling. If you are selling nationally, and you would not be a small enterprise if you were, and if you can afford the exorbitant rates of TV advertisements, then advertising on TV makes sense. But if your reach is much narrower, TV advertisements are only wasteful. If you are selling, say, only in one city, then the best way to advertise is through hoardings in that city, through slides or even videos shown in the city's cinema theatres, through pamphlets and through local newspapers.

While some forms of selling efforts create awareness and interest in the product and hence demand for it, others facilitate its availability. The former are called *pull factors*, because they pull the buyer to your product. The things like dealer discounts, 'schemes' and POP are *push factors* because they help you send more products through your distribution network. The point is that push and pull factors are both needed for a sustained selling campaign. They have to be done in a manner by which they complement each other in time and space. When you pull in Delhi, you must also push there, and not in some other place!

Planning for sales growth therefore needs an awareness of all the factors listed above. Each one of your moves has to be planned and designed to suit others. Obviously, the initial introduction of the product in a new geographic area needs a lot of money to be spent. But you must remember that in FMCG the failure rate is very high and if you need long-term success of your product and brand, you cannot be found wanting in it.

To an extent the various elements of the selling efforts may be made to substitute each other. This is what the lizard does: he offers retailers and distributors a deal they cannot refuse, say 10 per cent commission for distributors and 30 per cent for retailers. But then he will not give any POP, not have any publicity, no advertisement and so on. The incentive of a hefty commission makes the distribution network push the product hard. In initial stages Nirma followed this strategy but soon the lizard turned into a lion cub and had one of the most popular jingles heard on radio and TV.

Sometimes the lizard offers such a hefty commission that the retailer is willing to become a liar. This is quite commonly seen in our retailers. I remember that when some unknown brand of gulab jamun was introduced in Gujarat, retailers started saying that Amul has stopped production. That was patently false. Even now obscure brands of mosquito repellents are pushed by retailers saying that Good Knight is not available. Only when you start walking away do they reluctantly give it to you. The same things have happened when some competition appeared for Band Aid, for Electral and these days for the parenterals of Core. But these things do not always work and even more importantly, the retailer never agrees to any lower commission once he has tested this figure.

The matter of quality

Consistent with the way most manufacturers treat quality, I talk of quality at the very end in the list of important issues in the firm's growth. The most common operational view is: 'Well, quality is very important and we have the best quality control laboratory in the industry. But we do not reject bad lots, we send them to the customers who do not mind that quality.'

Honestly, is this what you do? Believe me the only thing which will separate the men from the boys in the small industry in the long run is their care and consistency in quality.

What is really meant by quality? The conventional definition is that it must meet the standards set in the ISI (or the FPO or the PFA) books for the relevant product. If, for example, for expeller groundnut oil, moisture must be lower than 0.25 per cent, FFA below 1.5 per cent, colour below 6, etc., and it should be free from extraneous matter, then your oil must meet the standards. Similarly, if a super-enamelled wire of 16 SWG must have thickness within a given range, must be able to meet a certain number of tests of toughness, malleability, heat resistance and insulations, then your wire must meet these standards. If your products meet ISI standards then your product has high quality.

Isn't this a negative way of looking at quality? Should one not say that my product will: (*a*) give the performance for which it is primarily meant for a period longer than a certain time: *and* (*b*) not cause any side effect which may cause material, financial or psychic damage to the user? Only that kind of a product is normally accepted as a product of good quality.

But the best and the brightest of the Indian companies are so doubtful of their product's quality that they refuse to accept any contingent liability. Those who do, use it as an advertising strategy.

A fan does not come to be known as a Crompton fan just because it meets some tests. Nor does Bajaj become Hamara Bajaj merely because their scooter meets ISI specifications, if any exist for that product. Crompton becomes a symbol of reliability and acquires a name, and with that the firm acquires the fame, because a Crompton fan virtually never stops working in peak summer or its blades fall out and hurt people or someone gets a shock putting it on under normal circumstances. Similarly, you do not buy a Bajaj scooter simply because it has been okayed in some tests but because you know that nothing much ever wrong goes with a Bajaj for as long as ten years of routinely heavy, almost negligent running.

Now, being able to guarantee performance is different from saying that it will meet ISI standards. And saying that the product will not cause any unintended consequence which damages the buyer in any way is an even tougher definition. But some such tough definition is implicit in the way the quality guru Taguchi views it: 'Quality is the net loss which the unintended effects of the product cause on the buyer and the society.'

If driving after a couple of pegs of whisky leads you to an accident, it is not a problem of quality. If any thing, it shows that the whisky had 'authority'. But if you get stomach upsets, headaches or any medical problem because of admixtures in it, then the whisky was of dubious quality. This is a shift—and a shift I advocate—from the goal-post approach of saying that the necessary parameters are within the ISI range.

Does improvement of quality necessarily mean higher cost? Well, it really depends on the way you look at it. If you insist on putting the most expensive ingredients/components/raw materials into your product because you believe that it is the only way to improve quality, the cost is bound to hit the sky. But it is perfectly possible to make a lousy end-product with the most expensive parts or materials. Even if you gave me the best of rice, nuts, raisins, spices and meats, I can make supremely inedible *biryani* out of them (try me if you wish). Conversely, for making a delicious and healthy *biryani*, one really does not need the most exotic ingredients.

The quality of the end-product is a function of the product design vis-a-vis its most common operating environment, also of component quality, inter-components compatibility *and* workmanship.

The typical operating environment in which a product is going to be used is beyond your control. However, what you can control are: product design, choice of the various components and the workmanship. Workmanship is more prone to variation as the same product is going to be made thousands of time and some human variations are inevitable. For controlling that you have quality control checks—in-process and at the final testing stage. These checks by themselves can do nothing at all to make the choice of the design and components mix a superior one in terms of cost-quality profile.

The current trend is to talk of sustained quality improvements through participative approaches. Inherent in these approaches is the spirit of positive experimentation with the product design and choice of components. In this way of looking at quality, sustained improvements in quality are possible only if:

- The in-process and final quality checks are separated from quality improvement efforts and grouped as strictly quality assurance;
- You keep trying out minor variations in design and try to use cheap components which still do not result in decreased overall performance; and
- Keep trying this combination involving people who are doing the job of manufacture.

This approach says that you should not believe that you are the only source of wisdom in the organisation. You must allow workers to try new things. Once the group of persons—you, your engineer, workers and production supervisor—all agree that the key to improved product quality lies in a critical list of processes and components, carefully designed experiments can give you the best combination possible at the least cost.

The most crucial thing is to recognise that it is a terribly short-sighted policy to sell whatever you are making (and hence finding out the poor wretched customer who can afford nothing better) rather than selling something you would like to buy for your purpose, something you would not be ashamed to give your wife on her birthday, something your children can proudly say is made by their father, something which will give customers value for money and more. And you need an open mind, a spirit of experimentation and the guts to invite the cooperation of even the lowest worker to help you improve the quality of your product. The products of high quality are never too expensive for the customers once they know that they are getting their money's worth.

9

Your People Form the Core

In the previous chapter, I offered suggestions about the four crucial dimensions of growth: management of sales growth, management of asset expansion, management of finances and management of quality. However, the core of every organisation is people, and there is no way you can transform the organisation from a small enterprise to a medium or large organisation without similarly transforming its people—including you.

There can be no magical metamorphosis. People themselves are not transformed. What is transformed is what they do in the organisation, how they do it, how they relate to each other, to the entrepreneur and to outsiders and the rules they use while deciding how to do these things.

When the organisation is really small, perhaps there are very few persons in it—just you, and a few workers. What happens then is that the workers do exactly *what* you tell them to do, even exactly *how* you say it. Often they may wait for you to come back and tell them what to do. They relate to you as your unquestioned and unquestioning subordinates. The simple rule is that what you say is right.

As long as their relationship with each other does not in any way affect the work, you do not worry about it. In other words they are merely faceless instances of a category, your *adami*, the horrible dehumanising way in which Hindi-speaking entrepreneurs describe their employees. As the organisation grows, all this needs to change.

Of course, most enterprises begin small. To begin with all the managerial functions are done by the entrepreneur himself. He may, more likely than not, make one of his relatively more skilled and trusted workers an informal boss of others. He may then add a foreman or a supervisor to supervise production in his absence and in the night shift. He still visits the factory in the second/night shift. (Often because he has not delegated any thing at all to the trusted worker and sometimes because of an oft-repeated comment which becomes a self-fulfilling prophecy: 'You just cannot trust their work when I am absent. If I want good output I must be there.')

Then comes a stage when he must hire an accountant. The entrepreneur takes care of marketing and customer relations, the foreman takes care of production and the accountant does the rest. This trio of boss-foreman-accountant continues for quite sometime as the firm grows. For a long time, the accountant also doubles as the administration and personnel man. Finally, when the firm is about to start its transition to a medium-scale unit, the boss starts needing someone who can reinforce and follow up on his selling efforts and he picks up a salesman. This, then, is the usual way people are added to a small organisation.

While men have been added to the firm, decision-making remains centralised. Most often, since all the figures and facts are in the boss's head, there is virtually no record of any kind. The lizard entrepreneur does not even keep good accounting records. There may be some accounting record if the boss is not keen on 'informal' business (Blunders 3 and 4). He may also keep some rudimentary personnel records if he has an active social conscience and abides by labour laws. The point is, there is no formalisation; decisions are centralised, taken without recourse to much discussions between individuals involved, virtually no data analysis is done and the style of functioning is personalised.

Sustainable growth needs all if not most of this to change. And that is the most difficult part of the growth process. If a unit is making 100 pieces a month, the management process required to enable it to make 1,000 pieces per month is quite different *qualitatively*. Usually three things happen in this phase:

- To manage the larger scale of operations, new and qualitatively different individuals are inducted into the firm;

- A part of the decision-making process becomes more organised and formalised, needing analytical inputs using data (which needs to be repeatedly generated and hence maintained), as well as judgemental inputs based on perceptions of many rather than one individual; and
- An unintended group dynamics almost completely beyond the control of the boss sets in as the decision-making process gets under way and gathers force.

Consequently, in myriad different variations, issues of organisational culture, sustenance and development start becoming repeatedly important. And most frequently the bottom line of all discussions in such organisations in flux is the same: we know we can do things better, faster and cheaper, if only the boss will let us do our work. If you have the ambition to transform the firm from a small roadside enterprise to a large and vibrant industrial giant, you need a carefully decided plan to make yourself redundant in *day to day, routine and repetitive action* in your organisation in a short span of time, without really affecting the volume or the quality of the output.

This chapter offers you hints on how to do it. The best role for you is also discussed. A word of warning: Trying to do it just like what I write is trying to do those ghastly callisthenics by just watching TV fitness programmes. Invariably, this is the process which needs outside help, and after all what are good consultants for?

What follows in this chapter are: suggestions on how to introduce systems of communication, authority flow and control in the organisation; how to help older employees cope with these changes without feeling deliberately slighted; and how to make yourself redundant. I will also suggest what you need to do with yourself when you have made yourself redundant in routine affairs, that is, what should be your role and how best to perform it.

Systems at work

It is necessary to carefully understand the meaning of certain words. *Routine* actions are those which are done time and again, every day, repeatedly, in a nearly identical manner, leading to predictable consequences. (A household illustration: To make the cup of tea which brings a smile to your wife's face, take two cups of water, grate a quarter-inch piece of ginger in it, set it to boil, add three teaspoons of sugar. When it starts simmering, add two spoons of Brooke Bond Red Label tea, boil for half a minute, cover the pot, add a little warm milk after two minutes and filter. Well, that is routine.) Hence, routine matters are those which involve basically mundane actions.

There may be occasions when in routine matters, a decision has to be taken between two sets of independent routine actions. (Another household example: when a guest arrives, you decide whether to offer him a lemonade or a cup of tea. While the decision may need the input of desire from the guest, it is a routine matter and the choice is between two independent actions both of which are absolutely routine.)

As opposed to routine actions and matters, *discretionary matters* are those in which a careful assessment of several, including new factors, needs to be made; using the specialised skill of judgement available with (or allowed to) only a few and the consequences of which action cannot be precisely predicted. The relatively less predictability of the consequences makes the discretionary matters critical.

For example, there is a tender for supplying products which you make. How much to quote, what delivery periods to offer, etc., are discretionary matters (and so is the matter of how much to bribe, unless the relevant department has made clear-cut conventions of 2 per cent of order value or some such thing). Such decisions cannot be left to every one, and the discretion to decide is restricted to only a few.

This is the situation where the discretion is restricted by the management's choice. In some situations, judgement about what needs to be done in a given situation has to be made by some one who has special education, training and experience for doing so. What dose of anaesthesia is to be given to a particular patient is not decided by even the surgeon, leave alone the owner of a private hospital. It requires the special training and experience of an anesthetist. This is the situation of a skill-based discretion available to a professional.

Commercial organisations have got to function by performing all actions efficiently and at minimum cost. Since discretionary matters require consideration of relevant facts, analysis and judgement of a professional, such decisions take time. The organisations which allow a whole lot of actions to remain discretionary never become very efficient or economical. Allowing routine actions to be decided in a discretionary format is wasteful and foolish. A whole household cannot debate how much sugar to put in their morning tea every day. Hence the trick is to maximise the scope of routine actions and ensure that they are done routinely. In fact, it is desirable to move some of the discretionary actions into the fold of the routine.

What is introduction of systems in an organisation? Contrary to popular misinterpretation of the word 'systems', inherently, it has little to do with computerisation. For an organisation which has no formal systems in place, attempting to computerise things is somewhat like trying to give vitamins to a patient who is basically starving for want of food.

Introduction of systems involves four things:

- Careful categorisation of all actions into routine and discretionary;
- Laying down detailed and foolproof instructions for all routine matters, instructions which, if followed, can never lead to unwanted results;
- Establishing procedures to ensure that the instructions regarding routines are, in fact, followed by those who are involved; and
- Defining the manner in which discretionary matters will be dealt with.

In fact, the entrepreneur becomes redundant in routine actions only when he sets systems at work which no longer require his decision on most matters. And making the top boss redundant in day-to-day running of the organisation is the primary goal of introduction of systems.

Identification of routine and discretionary matters

For doing this, you might like to make a quick inventory of all that you and your colleagues do in the organisation. For example, you buy raw materials and components. How do you do it? When do you do it? How much of each item is bought at one go? How do you decide from whom to buy? Do you pay an advance? Is there a cut given to you in cash? How much? How do you pay? After how many days? Who is paid on priority? Are all items bought in the same manner? At what frequency and in what manner do you follow up on orders?

Initially, answers to these and many more such questions in purchasing itself appear trivial to you. That is because you are doing it yourself. But suppose I were to join you, will I be able to do the purchasing without referring things to you? I could, but only if such things were carefully documented in the form of a manual or a ready reckoner of instructions.

There is no need to become utterly commonplace in these efforts to document, nor is it necessary to be unduly evasive. The extent of formalisation is to be defined by you. The central idea is that the actions which are routine need to be clearly identified and actions which require discretion need to be emphatically and unmistakably made known to the operating people.

(Imagine the chaos if you wrote in your document that the suppliers of stationery and general items are to be stretched and paid at least three months after supply, and this is revealed by an idiot clerk to them! Or even worse, if you enter in the records that usually the supplier of ferro-silicon gives three per cent in cash back to you? So, obviously, everything cannot be written up.)

Laying down foolproof procedures for routine action

The procedures for performance of routine actions must be written down in complete detail, missing no aspect however small. This is the only way you actually avoid the need for any one to keep making routine things a matter of discussion. An illustration for the recording of incoming and outgoing mail is given in Box 9.1.

> **BOX 9.1**
> **Instructions for the dispatch clerk**
>
> *For incoming mail*
>
> 1. Ensure that the date on the 'Received' stamp is the current date.
> 2. For all incoming letters originating from outside the firm, please put the 'Received' stamp on the letter.
> 3. Enter for each incoming letter originating from outside the firm in the Outside Mail Register the following details in the appropriate columns:
>
>   Serial number
>   Name and designation of sender
>   Short postal address
>   Date of the letter as mentioned in it
>   Date of receipt in the office
>   Person to whom marked
>
> 4. Please note that the serial number of the letter will be entered on the letter itself on the top right column of the first page.
> 5. Whenever the sender addresses the letter to a specific officer by name, the letter should be marked to him. For all other letters and in all cases when instructed, the letters are to be marked to the PA to MD.

Once these procedures are laid down and generally learnt, the chances of error are minimised. Further, whenever there is any argument about the quality of performance, the exact step in which a worker committed the mistake can be identified and relevant training given.

Laying down procedures for routine actions may seem wasteful to you. After all, you feel that your organisation is very small and why should you saddle it with so much paperwork? If you are missing the point, do this to begin with on a matter which you feel is very routine but always takes a long time to get done.

You will discover one of these three facts, none of which is pleasant: By denying that actions are routine and claiming that your instructions are needed in each of the matters, (*i*) either your subordinates are shirking work, or (*ii*) you as a team are inefficient, or (*iii*) you have created a situation of utterly inadequate delegation.

Let us look at the third possibility first. If you have hired cheap Harirams, then their self-perception is quite poor to start with. You also think that they really are incompetent. You feel that unless you tell them what to do and exactly how to do things, they will never be able to do anything worthwhile. So you keep interfering. Whatever and however the fellow is doing, you keep giving instructions, necessary or otherwise. If he does something right in your absence, you express obviously patronising surprise: '*Arre wah, Hariram, tu to bahut hoshiyar ban gaya!*'(Wow, Hariram! You've really become clever!)

If he makes even the slightest error, you come down hard on him, saying that you have always felt that the fellow was useless, but you thought he could do at least *this* after being given instructions for it a hundred times, and does the fellow never feel that the heavy object on his shoulders is his head meant to be used some times and ... you get the idea. There is every likelihood that you have done this to some defenceless creature. The frustrations of running small enterprises are so many; you have got to take out your anger somewhere.

Any way, what happens as a result? No one takes any initiative in doing anything at all. Unless they are told what to do and exactly how to do it, they simply wait. If you are absent at the time, well, it remains pending. Then more work comes and some of that keeps pending, the rest just accumulates. And so on. The delegation of work becomes completely non-functional. Eventually, what you consider routine, and what actually is routine, takes an unduly long time to get done. Here, you must realise that the source of the problem is you.

The first possibility is that your subordinates are using absence of instructions as a pretext to shirk work. This will certainly happen with those who have been assigned a lot of varied, but drab and dull routine work. Since they are required to do many things, their priorities become either what has just been told as urgent or, more likely, what they think will please the boss.

The last is the most dangerous in the long run, but of that some other time. The point is that while to you it is as yet just a feeling that things are routinised, the subordinate is perhaps in a position to think up some reason why your specific instruction was needed and hence did not do the job. Only when you put down every detail carefully in the form of procedures, the subordinate no longer has the excuse of needing instructions. Why, then, even the fact that you have given him too many things to do might actually get discovered.

The active possibility that you are a hopelessly inefficient team is hopefully small. What is more likely is that you are disorganised, you do not have a proper system of work and hence on every thing you end up spending more time than you need to. Again, back to systems, is it not?

Establishing procedures for follow-up

This is relatively simple. All you have to do is make a surprise check once in a while and see that people are following the procedures that have been laid down. When these procedures are new, checks should be more frequent. That the people have, in fact, understood the procedures and feel at home with them (both, skill wise and feeling wise) has to be verified by seeing what they make of them. Any kinks in these procedures need to be set right. But once in action, an occasional check with strong enough reprimand for default should meet the case.

In truly family-managed organisations, things are usually hopelessly informal and when systems are attempted, everyone feels that he is so close to the boss that the systems are not really meant for him, but only for others. Rigorous implementation of formal procedures becomes very difficult. Sometimes this difficulty is exacerbated by the behaviour of the boss. An example is given in Box 9.2.

BOX 9.2
Procedures and the boss

In my first job, the boss encouraged every one to keep meeting him. No wonder, most of his time was spent talking to others on a strictly informal basis. Shy people stayed out even when they

> had important work because they saw that he was busy with others. So work suffered. When he discovered that, he introduced the procedure that any one wishing to see him had to meet his PA, explain to her the purpose of the meeting and meet him only when she allowed.
>
> I was neither very dashing nor very popular with the PA and so after this procedure was put in effect I did not see the boss for a whole fortnight. Guess what he said when he first met me afterwards? 'What is wrong with you? I hardly see you nowadays. Is there anything wrong? Come and just chat whenever you feel like.' I told him that I had wanted to see him for the last one week, but the PA did not send me in at all. He then turned back to me and said, 'Good God, don't tell me that you are taking those procedures seriously? Why, nobody else does!'
>
> Now, that is the funny thing about procedures. I hope the message is clear to you.

Defining the way to deal with discretionary matters

All that is not routine is discretionary, right? Well almost, but that is not the way one would wish it. There is the intermediate stage of part-judgemental and rest routine. That needs to be disposed of first. In such matters what needs to be done is that the points at which judgement is needed should be separated and clear instructions on whose job and responsibility it is to give that judgement should be issued. The rest is routine. For example, instructions for the officer in charge of dispatching goods to buyers can be:

'If on any day the quantity of some item manufactured is smaller than what the buyer listed in the dispatch schedule has asked, the officer shall ask the marketing manager whether:

- Part lots are to be dispatched; or
- The lot is to be held back till the time the remaining quantities are manufactured; or
- The dispatches are to be made to some other buyer against his orders.

The actual dispatches will be effected according to the orders of the marketing manager. In case he is absent, then the first option is to be chosen, if the remaining goods will take more than one day to be made, otherwise the second or third option is advisable.'

Matters which are purely discretionary are always troublesome to handle. The pertinent questions are: who is to be given discretionary powers, what are the limits of these powers, how is one to separate the areas of technical discretion and of financial/policy discretion as to make the procedures functional, how does one balance the need for control on what goes on in the organisation and the need for discretion? You may rest assured that these are difficult questions to which not you alone but a lot of people are groping for answers. It will be audacious and self-defeating for me to give answers to all these and similar questions. Audacious because the situation faced by each firm is unique and needs careful tailor-made answers. And self-defeating because this is the way many consultants make their living.

Some systems are special

And among them the most special are the management control systems. They need to be handled most carefully. The only reason I am mentioning them here is to try and give you a flavour of the complexity of what is involved so as to prevent you from stretching your feeling of omniscience into trying something amateurish and ill thought.

The set of questions regarding discretion in the last paragraph is close to the core of management control systems. The basic purpose of management control systems is to ensure that:

- Performance in the organisation is, in fact, moving in the desired direction;
- Material and money resources are used in a judicious and productive manner; and
- Responsibility for performance can be accurately pinpointed and that there are adequate morale-boosting measures of recognising and rewarding good performance.

Management control systems presume that the organisation knows its objectives fairly clearly, that it understands the process by which these objectives are being achieved, that it can design ways of measuring the performance, that all wrong or deviant acts can be detected and corrected, and that it can design reward systems for encouraging better performance.

These assumptions are in an area which is almost always deceptive. Firms and entrepreneurs always believe that they know their objectives even when, in fact, there is a degree of imprecision or confusion about them. They believe that they understand the processes involved, when often they do not. They feel that performance can be accurately measured and that they are actually measuring it, while frankly nothing of the kind is happening. They feel that they are able to spot good performers and are rewarding them well, while in reality they may be falling prey to plain sycophancy. They feel that deviant action is seen and corrected quickly, while the problems are there. In informally managed small enterprises, the control systems are usually out of tune with the need and the reality.

The general principles of a good management control system are indicated in the following questions:

- Does the firm have a single or multiple objectives?
- Is there complete agreement on objectives between major players of top management (all partners, for example)?
- Are these objectives stable or rapidly changing?
- Are the methods for undertaking the purchase, production and marketing clearly understood?
- Are the results of these actions completely predictable or are there major factors outside the control of the firm which crucially affect the performance (e.g., prices, foreign exchange rates, power supply, labour availability, transportation, etc.)?
- Are the basic activities expected of staff to be controlled clear and repetitive?
- Are there clear relationships between inputs and outputs, relationships which are not dependent upon the outside factors listed above (for example, so many kilos of oil per MT of oil seeds, so much use of steam, power and chemicals per MT)?

- Is there a broad measure of agreement on these relationships?

If you claim to have understood the full significance of these questions in the context of your firm, write about it to me. If you have not, congratulations, you are honest, and if you need help, you can still call me.

It is mentioned particularly with the view to help your poor helpless employees whom you may be controlling inappropriately that quantitative norms for inputs use or tight budgetary controls are justifiable only if:

- The objectives are precisely known, and the relationships between actions and their results are predictable;
- All external factors have been adequately provided or alternatively the employees' tasks insulated from them;
- Priorities of performance expectation are not changed; and
- The actions involved are repetitive.

The situations which satisfy all the four conditions are quite infrequent and so I hope that the entrepreneurs will be less adamant about imposing quantitative norms on their employees.

The end result of introducing systems

On the positive side of the end results there are some entries. Every one knows whose job is to do primarily what. Gaps (that is the tasks left to Mr Nobody and hence not done at all) are clearly identified and it is possible to give more attention to them. Everyone knows exactly how these tasks are to be done. They will know to whom they are to report what, when and how frequently. They know who will authorise what, how and when. They will know what is expected of them. They will hopefully also know what they may expect. Wasteful meetings and discussions are avoided. Wholly unintended alibis for poor performance and loopholes or ambiguities for corruption or wastage are eliminated. Time required per unit of action comes down. You get a better idea of what is the sustainable level of performance in your organisation. Scaling up becomes possible.

There are a lot of entries on the negative side. You individually lose a lot of control. You have got to behave much more reasonably and responsibly. If you are doing things on the side or making money in some manner, it is easily exposed or exposable. Demands for putting facilities (such as a generator set) in place or hiring people gain visibility and strong support from exposed facts. Also, people who felt a sense of personal involvement get at least temporarily a little upset. Some might feel angry at the loss of their hitherto omniscient power. Other might feel deliberately ignored and neglected. General costs of staff are likely to slightly increase in the short run.

Balance the pros and cons. Think how keen you are on growing and decide whether you have to have systems, at what pace and in which areas.

And what shall I do with my people?

A chap who almost became my client once told me of his growth ambitions and plans. He said that while his plans were feasible in terms of material and money resources, it was the people who were the basic constraints. They had been with his father when *he* started the business some four decades ago. They stayed with him through good days and bad days. They were like a part of an extended family. And he went along the familiar lines of how some of them are not well educated, cannot get other jobs at that age and so on.

Then he took out two letterheads. One was smudged, badly printed and looked fairly cheap. The other was on some expensive imported paper, was embossed and had a touch of class about it. What he said then was that his people were really fit only to use the cheap letterhead. And now he had to use the better letterhead for his new business plans. What could he do to make them become able to even write their names on it?

This is the most challenging and troublesome aspect of growth. The problem is severe for those who have operated in the lizard mode for many years. It is much less severe for the lion cubs, mainly because their firms are relatively younger, and so would be most of the staff. But systematisation for growth poses some other problems for them.

Let us first look at the problems which a lizard, all set to grow, faces in regard to his people. It would be surprising if he had not committed Blunders 4 (operating informally), 5 (spawning too many dummy firms), 6 (selling whatever he produces in the shortage-ridden economy) and 7 (hiring cheap employees). Conjure up the image of this business.

For years, the boss has been cutting all sorts of corners to save that extra rupee. He has been engaging in very extensive 'persuasion' (or, after the Enron controversy, 'education') of the regulators. He has been deriving much work out of ill-trained colleagues. They are mostly Harirams from within the lizard clan or from families of very poor social and economic status.

He has kept his formal records to a minimum. He retains all decisions in his hands, the bulk of the staff usually comprising yes-men. The louder a man says yes, the better he is felt to be. Trustworthiness and loyalty and their willingness to put in long hours have so far been the criteria for deciding who is better among the yes-men. But now the lizard wants to make his firm grow into a large organisation. And that does not mean just a public issue.

(For some collateral reasons the flotation of a public issue somehow signifies to both insiders and outsiders that the firm is 'modernising'. These reasons are not far to seek. A public limited company has to have much greater transparency. Perhaps, along with the public issue there is a foreign collaboration or a significant expansion with money from respectable outfits like IDBI and not just the State Vikas Nigams. These people presumably need systematic work so alien to the lizard's working environment all this while. The public issue happens to coincide with a sea-change in the firm's working pattern. The lizard at least begins to shed its skin.)

The problems regarding people are several. In the first place, the overall abilities of the existing people have to be enhanced. In the second place, the work habits of the employees *and of the boss* have to change. In the third place, the inevitable but painful differentiation among existing people has to be implemented. This subsumes the necessary task of providing emotional as well as financial sops to those who have to be either cut to size or even sent on pension. In the fourth place, new people have to be attracted, inducted, retained and encultured in the organisation. In the fifth place, the group dynamics between the 'old faithful' and the new has to be sorted out. And all this has to be accomplished without allowing the pace of production, marketing or expansion to suffer.

Differentiating and relocating people

From the star pattern of the organisation, as your firm grows, it starts having a 'structure', with clear demarcated lines of authority and communications. You cannot be hiring new people for all the supervisory or managerial roles. Many insiders have to be utilised in new, perhaps higher positions. The question is who becomes the supervisor of which other fellow. Doing this by seniority is one old way, but you know the pitfalls of that. So you have to now assess the people strictly on merit.

You need to look at their abilities, contributions, loyalty and of course potential. And that means, essentially a process of judging. You need to be careful as you cannot afford to anger any one so badly as to make him leave you. After all, the lizard in the next den is hoping to steal your people and business. It may be a good idea to involve all your people in the process of assessment and relocation. May be an outsider could be called in to do the job for you. The process not only must be fair but also *seem* to be fair.

Enhancing abilities

Skills, knowledge and attitudes together combine to form functional abilities of people with regard to work.

Skills are basically the habits of manoeuvering machines and objects and controlling one's own body movements for producing desired results. If the firm in its new form is going to need different processes, machinery, techniques and office aids, the existing staff has to learn to use these efficiently. Such new equipments may include computers, fax, EPABX, e-mail, NC lathe, new QC equipments, new processing vats, new packing machines and so on. All these require skills which the workers did not possess so far. People are not expected to learn these automatically. Efforts have to be made to teach them these new skills and make them feel comfortable using new machinery. Sometimes inducements have to be offered to make them feel interested in the new set-up. Some are born enthusiastic learners, while others combine learning with sullen attitudes. Each has to be handled in his own way.

Knowledge is the sum total of facts and relationships between facts and their causation in relation to the work at hand. During the growth phase firms seldom have the luxury to expand the knowledge base of their staff. They prefer recruitment of those who know. But usually, the knowledge base of employees is best expanded by sending them to training programmes of technical or managerial nature at professional training institutions.

In this context *attitudes* refer to the unthinking responses and immediate reactions to things like other people, value of time, quality of the product, precision, material use and aesthetics. The usual attitudes one encounters in introducing systems of work or other modern ways of doing things is one of sullen, defensive reluctance. Among the employees, there is a grudging acceptance of the fact that their current ways will not work for a larger outfit. They also feel that the systems may be a better solution. Hence they do not feel like rejecting the new things out of hand.

But there is a lurking suspicion in their mind that the acceptance of new things by the boss is born out of his unfavourable judgement regarding *their* ability. And all this while they had been doing exactly what the boss had told them. So they seem to suggest, 'How can he hold us responsible and blame us?' The fact, of course, is that they are certainly not to be blamed.

Acceptance of doing things in a formal and proper way is no reflection on the ability, loyalty or trustworthiness of the existing staff. Yet this is what they perceive. So a lot of kid-glove treatment is needed. Unfortunately, since it is simpler to find fault with the poor defenceless subordinates than with oneself, many entrepreneurs become rather loud in their contemptuous dismissal of the older staff during the process of modernisation. That certainly does not help.

In general, therefore, the abilities of the team as a whole are enhanced by intervening in these three forms:

- Specific job-oriented training for skill upgradation of the relevant workers;
- Longer duration training programmes for improvement of knowledge base of some chosen (and obviously senior) managerial personnel; and
- Inputs targeted at team building and motivation.

Apart from the (largely hoped for but not always certain) favourable consequences of these interventions on the actual abilities of the team, a major favourable impact is felt on the perceptions of the people. They begin realising that the boss is serious about helping them cope with the changed situation. This is no mean achievement.

Changing work habits

The changes from informal to formal ways of doing work do not come automatically. There is always this kind of question in the minds of people: 'We have managed fine all these days doing things our way. Why do we now need all these systems suddenly?' This question is born out of genuinely insufficient appreciation of the systems and mainly out of the reluctance to change.

After all, when the firm was in the lizard mode, the employee never had to think on his own. He always came to the boss, asked him what was to be done, listened to his jibes and persiflage and did precisely as he was told. Now two things happen. First, he is expected to know what needs to be done as the work of systems design subsumes division of work in routine and non-routine matters and provides instructions to every one about almost everything. Second, even if he is doubtful, he is expected to consult the manual of instructions, something he is not comfortable with, or worse still ask that bright young engineer who joined 'last Tuesday'. The last really hurts. All this while, he went running to the boss when in doubt, so what if the boss shouted at him. Now this new chap makes him feel small and ignorant. Naturally he starts feeling as if he is deliberately slighted.

The changes in work habits can be irritating even for you. Work systematisation implies drawing of boundaries around what each one of you, including you yourself, are expected to do. No longer can you have as unfettered a way in your own firm. If you still behave in the old way, your managers start feeling deliberately slighted!

Inducting new people

There are four specific issues involved in inducting new people. The first is to attract whom you think are good people, which would presumably mean well-trained persons, doing well in life, having great potential, sound judgement and plenty of initiative. If you are a lizard, you will find this difficult except when you catch them real young. If you are badly located, then you might have a problem. While there is severe unemployment in the country, good people have plenty of options and are not easily available.

The second issue is to design a pay package which the trained people find attractive, the older lot do not find upsetting and you find affordable. The oldies invariably argue: 'We have been with you all these years, and you give us only so much and look at the new fellow.' You can, of course, tell them that this is the way it is going to be and they better like it. But remember, for your existing level of business, you need them. Only when your new facilities are ready, they can be dispensed with. Anyway, 'off with their heads' is feasible only in fiction.

There are two better options. The one I recommend is to offer a bit of equity, as a 'token of your appreciation of their loyalty'. Do it in a manner that does justice to the level of the employee and his seniority. You offer this to only old people with the explicit understanding that it compensates them for their years of service and that from now on you are free to design a pay package for the new fellows as you please. However, Employee Share Ownership Plans (ESOP) are not very common or popular in India. (An alternative, of the same basic type, the one that will definitely meet some appreciation is to divide your farmhouse in residential plots, sell it to them at low prices and also make the company give them loans for it.)

The second, more undesirable option, is to give something to the new fellows in 'a cash envelope', how much being known only to you and the new chap. This is a fairly common practice, though it is both illegal and immoral. Also, sooner rather than later, this comes to be known to the rest of the staff and then you are back to square one.

The third issue is enculturing them in your firm or at least making them feel comfortable. If you have been rather free with Blunder 7 then you have a lot of Harirams of the lizard clan or from among your social contacts floating around. The newcomer feels awkward. He feels obliged to be as servile with you and (other members of your family) as the Harirams are and, at the same time, feels a sense of irritation at the foolishness. He does not last. Often, even with the best pay package you can afford, you find it difficult to retain good fellows simply because they do not wish to be equated with the Harirams. The best policy to follow in this situation is to bring some one who does not speak the language at all (get a Tamilian if you are a dominantly Bengali firm, for instance). The need to communicate more formally with him in a different language automatically makes the Harirams more polite and proper with him.

Handling group dynamics

There is bound to be some amount of dynamics whenever there is a group. But as long as you were a small firm with a sharp star pattern of communication and authority, the group dynamics was too subdued to have any nuisance value. As you become more remote from routine and hence from where the bulk of the people are, the group dynamics gains intensity. It could start being manifested in any form (production vs marketing, factory vs office, workers vs staff, Marathis vs Agarwals, etc.).

People suddenly become aware of the fact that with the introduction of systems and increase in work flow, there is a greater absolute power available. Also, to make things independent of you, you personally do not give commands, but through some one else. Hence the question is who shall have that power. This business of power, as a Republican Senator from the USA once put it, is somewhat like sex. Every one feels that there is more fun in it than they actually get and they feel that the other fellow is having all the fun.

The tragedy is that this group dynamics can effectively undo what systematisation does. When one individual misbehaves you could straighten him but when a whole department or a large group of people are not cooperative, things get tough. For this purpose, you have to retain a measure of direct touch with the key operating people at every level as well as with potential troublemakers.

But what shall I do from now on?

Routine work is comforting. Your body as well as mind are occupied. When people come for instructions and reprimand, you get a sense of control, a feeling of being in the driver's seat. You also feel more comfortable and secure as, often, you really do not trust the others. When you put systems of work in place, it becomes possible for routine work (such as purchase, sales, production and bank relations) to go on without you. You become separated from the routine. Initially you may experience a vacuum in life. You may not know what to do with yourself. So the question 'But what shall I do from now on?' is quite likely to arise in your mind. The answer is to be found in a fascinating book called *Functions of the Executive* written by C. Barnard. The critical points of that book are summarised below followed by a discussion on what is expected of a good CEO.

Organisations are made of small operating units; for example, a typical dairy could have an accounts section, a reception dock, a sales depot, a personnel office and so on. Each one of these small units have highly specialised tasks which need to be carried out properly and promptly so as to make the organisation work efficiently. To begin with, most managers are given charge of one of these small operating units, but since you did not have a formal structure earlier, *you* were the manager of all the units.

The person now managing each unit has to acquire the necessary technical abilities and a thorough familiarity with the proper ways of performance in a particular unit. Both these skills are valuable but are somewhat narrow in their applicability. As a manager moves up the hierarchy he begins to control more and more small operating units. As such, on one hand, he needs to be familiar with the routine work of each one of the small units in order to supervise their functioning and on the other hand he needs to develop a skill which is more complex yet distinct from the ones required by the supervisors of the small units.

Managing a system of small units needs a skill which is, in effect, more than just a sum of the skills required to manage each one of the small units. In other words, managing the whole is somewhat different from managing individual parts.

Even though the manager may become involved in more and more 'general management tasks' he may still have to perform some tasks which by themselves are not general management tasks. Thus, the managing director of a steel mill may, if an occasion demands, try to secure a large order for long products. While doing so he is performing a sales job. Other managers may get involved in supervision of production functions or maintenance of a complicated machinery. Again while doing so, they are not performing the general management job but doing a specific functional task.

Thus, every general manager has to perform some 'general management tasks' (executive functions) and some functional tasks (non-executive functions). For effective performance of an organisation, the performance of individual units needs to be properly intermeshed. Such a process of coordination needs a well-organised system of communication. This communication relates to timing, quantum, rate, etc. of the routine jobs which each one of the units must perform. This communication system may be compared with the central nervous system of the human body. The essential tasks of a general manager consist of ensuring that such a system of communication exists and performs well in the organisation.

Empirical research has demonstrated that whenever such a system of communication is weak or malfunctioning, the chances of failure of the organisation as a whole are high. To create this system of communication, a manager needs to create positions of authority which will receive, transfer and generate necessary communication. Large and formal organisations start with creation of positions even before an organisation comes into existence.

Such a system is often depicted through organisational charts which show the hierarchy and the lines of communication and command. Organisation theory prescribes the proper manner of creating such a hierarchy. However, the general manager's job is not confined to just the creation of such positions of authority. He must find out good people and put them in the appropriate positions.

It has been said that no employee is good or bad in himself; he can only be good or bad in a given position. It is because of this incompatibility between jobs and people that often organisations need to 'restructure', that is, bring about simultaneous changes in the positions of communication and assignments of personnel to these positions.

While after putting good people in proper places, much of the job of the manager is done, what is then needed is to ensure that these people and all other individuals involved in this organisation provide the services for which they were installed in the right places.

An employee is essentially a social being obtained for the purpose of the organisation by means of a contract. On that employee several demands are being simultaneously made. For example, he may be a father, a husband, a club secretary, a production manager, secretary of association of engineers, etc. That employee will have to meet all these demands placed on him. If he fails to meet these demands then he will fail either as a father or as the secretary of the club or in some other capacity. Consistent failure on many grounds will always lead to disgruntled and frustrated employees.

It is, therefore, necessary for the general manager to help the employees, in particular the people put in positions of communication, to meet the demands placed by the organisation in the context of the overall demands placed on that individual. Thus, while the manager in reality is concerned only with the organisation, in practice he must try to help his subordinates in matters which do not relate to the organisation directly. This is the 'friend-philosopher-guide' role.

It is mistakenly believed that one can run an organisation by simply paying the employees higher salaries and expecting them to become completely subservient to the organisation. It is true that poor pay from an organisation will act as a block for eliciting cooperation from people but it is equally true that however high the salary may be, no employee will forget everything else and become a slave to the organisation. Therefore, it is necessary to create incentives and inducements other than money which will influence the concerned employee to work for the organisation. The point is not to force the employee but to create a situation by which he himself feels that it is his duty to treat the organisation as being more important than his other demands.

Organisations try to inculcate a sense of commitment in their employees precisely for this purpose. The Army creates this commitment by evoking feelings of patriotism and simultaneously creating a sense of belonging among its soldiers. The Church relies upon faith as an instrument to motivate missionaries to devote their entire life. Dairy cooperatives have tried to gain commitment of their employees by emphasising the fact that these cooperatives benefit the rural poor. Thus, in each case, resort is taken to something which is beyond the mundane and the commercial. Even in commercial organisations, such a sense of commitment is attempted by trying to inculcate in the employees a certain sense of values (for example, the 'IBM way of life').

Since a higher purpose has to be evoked if a necessary commitment on the part of the employee is to be forthcoming, a crucial part of the job of the manager is to evolve a system of objectives and missions which in themselves are laudable and to which an employee is likely to feel committed. The employees' loyalty, in the sense of obtaining their commitment to the tasks and demands made by the organisation, is largely done through inculcating a sense of duty towards the objective once defined.

Inconsistent behaviour particularly from personnel occupying positions of communication leads to a lack of effective performance and must, therefore, be avoided. It is believed, particularly by those who rely on money as a way to obtain cooperation, that any deviant behaviour is to be controlled by severe punishments. This is known as 'Theory X' or a carrot-and-stick approach.

However, it is discovered soon that excessive reliance on this way is the surest way of getting mediocre and unimaginative personnel who are willing to jump through hoops every time the boss cracks the whip. Such an organisation rarely grows much. Thus, the belief today is to obtain loyalty by inculcating a sense of responsibility among the employees. Having done so, matching of subsequent actions of willing employees is to be done informally.

The system of formal communication and paperwork continues to exist. But a large part of the work, particularly under pressures of time and other emergencies, is done informally just by using the right words. This is because everybody understands and wants to perform whatever is necessary for meeting the purpose.

Four character attributes necessary for a general manager are:

- A complex morality;
- Maintaining a sense of responsibility to the organisation;
- Ability to maintain a high level of activity; and
- Possession of general and technical abilities for doing the above.

We have already talked about difficult demands being made on individuals. For the general manager the demands are many more, not only in the social setting because of his age, his position in society, etc., but also within the organisation. He must be in a position to be fair to all the operating units. He must also be able to ensure that his demands are not inconsistent with the needs of any individual unit. The general manager may owe his personal friendship to a particular unit because of his past association with the unit. The production manager who becomes the general manager in a dairy may have lasting friendship with his subordinates in the production unit. Even in an organisational sense he must be loyal towards them. However, the job of a general manager is to balance the various demands placed on him by different units and to decide something which is in the overall interest of the organisation. While doing so, he is bound to be viewed as disloyal by one of the many units, but this is a part of the job.

Responsibility refers to the dependability of the general manager in the overall context of the organisational job. If he succumbs particularly under conflicting demands to a particular code of behaviour, he is not paying due attention to the overall organisation work. Therefore, the ability of the manager to act responsibly when the pace of work is high and when conflicting demands are being made on him, is a critical virtue necessary for proper general management. This virtue can rarely be taught; it is acquired by experience. The crux of general management lies in the possession and development of such a virtue.

10

So How Does One Get it Right?

This chapter briefly recapitulates the previous nine, goes on to give some additional banana skins on which the entrepreneur can trip and indicates the steps for introducing desired changes. It also indicates the tasks for which you need external support and how to get it.

Recapitulation

This book has been prepared for those small industrialists who wish to become industrial giants and for prospective entrepreneurs. The book starts by stating that while success in industrial enterprises is a function of both prudent management and chance, failure can be made to order.

It then goes on to argue that in the changed economic environment, there are both challenges and opportunities for small industries. The withering away of the licence-permit-regulation regime has meant both good and bad things. The exclusive preserve of small industries, the so-called reserved list has shrunk massively, and there are pressures on it to shrink further. The anti-monopoly and anti-large industry bias has simply melted away. The MNCs are knocking on the doors of the markets. Only those products in which the local players enjoy advantage due to transportation costs will remain unbranded and offer scope to small industries. Virtually all other products will experience the emergence of powerful brands and hence consolidation. Thus, coming years will see a massive and qualitatively changed competition for the small industry. In this setting, growth is not a matter of ambition any more; it has become a categorical imperative.

In Part Two, the book focuses on eight actions of management which are (*i*) commonly seen in the pattern of management in the domestic small industry, and (*ii*) replete with risks of making the enterprise stagnate or even go under. These are called Blunders in Chapters 3 and 4. The word may appear too strong to some, but error is too bland and mistake connotes a slip of small consequence, while none of these actions have small consequences.

Blunder 1 is excessive or exclusive dependence of the firm on one buyer. The key problem is caused by complete dependence on the fortunes and behaviour of the exclusive buyer, lack of experience, contacts and expertise of dealing with others in the market and one-sided asset specificity. Ancillarisation is seen to be problematic. Even appointment of sole selling distributors entails Blunder 1. Dependence on a single buyer or distributor for anything over 40 per cent of the turnover is a clear symptom of the likely trouble. Diversification across products, buyers, markets and regions is recommended.

Blunder 2 is titled biting more than one can chew and has to deal with expansion of fixed assets before adequate working capital is provided for. Creation of fixed assets blocks scarce cash and thus reduces liquidity. The priority in managing finances should always be: staying liquid (that is being able to meet payments due today, this week or month), followed by staying solvent (being able to repay all debts within the due dates), followed by earning good returns, followed by being ready to face future production requirements. Blunder 2 violates these priorities and can at times cause a crippling liquidity crunch.

Blunder 3 deals with borrowing in cash markets for making speculative purchases. Cash borrowings need to be serviced in cash, and since the charges cannot be formally expensed off, they work out to be very expensive. They also tie up a part of the production capacity without adding to formal turnover and hence detracts from making the white books becoming impressive. In effect, cash borrowings have very high leverage associated with them. Incurring these for making speculative purchases is therefore courting disaster.

Blunder 4 is titled weaving a web of commercial deception and cautions against transacting much business informally. It is recognised that some informal business has become an unfortunate but unavoidable reality as one needs to grease the various palms constantly being stretched. Some cash is also required to make payments of interest in cash for cash borrowings. But any action which has an effect of reducing the turnover or profits to a sizable extent is bad in principle and short-sighted from a long-term growth point of view.

Blunder 5 deals with spawning (multiplying) several small firms basically to remain anonymous and evading the application of some law. This is a direct fall-out of the mercantile capitalist origin of the industry. The reason is again to do with the fact that this makes for small formal turnovers and profits and hence is myopic when viewed in the context of long-term growth. If spawning many firms is absolutely necessary, at least one of them should always be nurtured and made big.

Blunder 6 is called marketing myopia and deals with selling whatever one makes rather than making what the market and the customers really want. This is seen to be the result of the shortage-led mindset of the entrepreneur. In earlier times in this country, almost everything was in short supply and the customers had to buy what was available. This made many producers palm off whatever they made. Things are changing and consumers have greater choice now and such ploys will not work.

Blunder 7 deals with the tendency to hire employees for reasons other than their competence. This is a common practice in the small industry which makes do with ill-trained and poorly-paid staff, often hired from destitute or lower-middle class families from among the kinship network of the entrepreneur. Such cheap employees, the Harirams, turn out to be very expensive in the medium-term and positively harmful to the long-term growth of the company.

Blunder 8 deals with faulty planning of the projects and deals with cases where the financing arrangements have been derived completely from faulty plans. The case of particular importance is where seasonality, formalities of testing, regulation, etc., delay commercial sales substantially but the project plan fails to anticipate this.

I feel the reader-entrepreneur must try and assess for himself whether his enterprise shows any sign of these blunders. As stated earlier, if his enterprise shows evidence of more than five of these blunders, he is reaching a desperate stage. On the other hand if his enterprise shows less than two or three of these, he is fairly safe.

He needs to be concerned only if he wishes to make his enterprise a large, successful and vibrant industry. If he is aiming at 'voluntary sickness' for reasons of overall reduction in the family's tax liability or deliberate stretching of institutional debts or any such reasons, he need not worry. He is doing just fine.

Part Three offers suggestions and positive help in managing different aspects of the business. Chapter 5 deals with three critical components of financial managements: assessing the need of working capital, understanding and managing leverage, and understanding the range of options for generating finance. Other topics covered in this part are management of competition, understanding the strategic style one has unintentionally adopted and its implications for the business, managing the growth process, and undertaking a restructuring of the business for take-off into a phase of sustained growth. The chapter on growth process deals with crucial concepts of managing asset expansion with sales growth and planning for sustainable sales growth. The chapter on restructuring is called 'Your People Form the Core' and deals in detail with issues of changing the style of working in the organisation without adversely affecting the people who have helped you come up.

Some additional points to note

The points discussed below are the result of years of observing the way of doing business in some enterprises, though these practices are becoming less common.

The first point concerns spreading oneself too thin. This is the classical Indian mercantile-capitalist style of business. For example, a young industrialist and his family I know, are simultaneously engaged in a small construction business, a pharmaceutical formulation unit, a mini rolling mill and a finance company. When last heard he was keen on setting up a solvent-extraction unit.

Often, business families start different activities like this from two motives. The first is pure experimentation. They are not sure which is the most appropriate and profitable line and so they try three or four. The one which works out is continued and others are sold off or closed. The second motive is to ensure that each one of their children has something of his own to manage. Thus, one son, Raju, manages Raju Constructions, the other son, Ashok, manages Ashok Vitamins and the son-in-law, Dinesh, runs Goswami Rolling Mill. After *Babuji* goes to the heaven, these three businesses will separate and be run independently.

There is, of course, sound logic in doing this for either of the two reasons. While spawning many firms in general is not too bright an idea in manufacturing firms, it appears to be perfectly fine for trading houses. The reason is despite their formal names, for all one knows, in the business fraternity the firms may be called Gokulchand Dewanchand or some such thing, the name coming from the father or the grandfather of the present patron. Separate businesses for each son means that they will have enough operating space and can learn to do business in their own firm, without getting under the feet of other siblings. And experimentation before finally settling down to one line is eminently prudent.

It would be fine if these were the motives and if the experimentation is short-lived. But my friend referred to above has been running all his disparate businesses for decades, none of them are doing too well and he is harassed all the time. There is the problem of over-diversification, spreading oneself too thin, etc. In any case, one should not forget that in the process of setting up many firms, all of them will remain small and stunted. And if their businesses are as far removed from each other as building construction and formulations of vitamins, then there will be no *synergy* between them. (Synergy is that quality or strength of the business which helps many business lines and reduces costs or improves the competitive ability in those lines.) My point, therefore, is that if for the reasons listed above you have to spawn many firms, at least do them in related businesses so that you will get some advantages of shared learning and synergy.

The second point concerns the rather common tendency of *stretching institutional finances by different means*. Again the point is not moral but eminently practical. Suppose you have got a financial assistance and loan from the State Vitta Nigam for setting up your small industry to make, say, biscuits. You may have done well or not so well, forget the matter. But you took your time in repaying the loan. You stretched the Nigam, they issued you notices, you were declared a defaulter and the matter went into a protracted negotiation for settling the loan. Even assuming that you used their money perfectly legitimately and, commercially, yours was a sound venture. What is the problem?

From the growth point of view, say, you now wish to become a big industrialist and are negotiating loans from one of the National FIs, not merely a State Vitta Nigam. What then happens is that as a routine part of their appraisal of your loan application, they ask for your previous record of institutional finance. They do this even if you are one of the chief promoters, not even the key person. And then this business of your having become a defaulter and so on comes out. Unless you have managed to wash that with very solid performance thereafter, out goes your application. So it is always best to try and stay on the right side of the repayment performance.

The third and the final point concerns treatment of employees and suppliers. It is commonly known that most of the industrialists treat their customers very well. And that is for the simple reason that the customers give them business and if not treated well, they will go to someone else. That is well recognised. What about the employees and the suppliers?

Wherever the law does not compel the employers to do something for the workers and the employees, the chances are that it will not be done. It is remarkable that in Japan where bankruptcy rates of enterprises are among the highest in the world, retrenchment rates are not! And Japanese firms have a great problem dumping a supplier with whom they have had business association in the past.

While it is possible to argue that for a labour-surplus economy, India has ultra-labour friendly laws and that if the industrial unit pays all that is legally due to the employees he will become unviable (two of the commonest comments on this subject from the small industrialists I know), the fact remains that when it comes to employee relations and management the small industrialist is less than sympathetic. Even granting the economic compulsions for scrounging on employee benefits, the question of overall treatment of the employee remains. Details are not necessary, suffice it to say that enlightened thought recommends that you treat your employees with the same consideration you lavish on your customers. And as you sow, so shall you reap. The same is valid for your suppliers with even greater force.

Where do you need help?

The entrepreneur is convinced that if he does not understand a given technology, he must hire a technical consultant to show him the ropes. Also, if he cannot manage the mind-boggling sales tax, excise, income tax and labour-related records, he hires outside help for these purposes.

I submit that the entrepreneur needs to consult other entrepreneurs and well-wishers who can act as sounding boards for him during the transition and growth period. A small entrepreneur acts as an unquestioned boss in his unit and no one dares stop or defy him. Yet we saw earlier, many decisions taken by him are just plain blunders. How is he to avoid making such blunders? By asking someone who understands business, whom the entrepreneur regards as enlightened and progressive. Possibly another successful entrepreneur, may be the secretary of the local industries association or the buyer of the large company with whom he constantly deals. The best thing could be that the industry association starts periodic meetings for free discussions among members for their concerns of this nature. The main thing is that the sounding board role should be performed by someone who is not dependent on the entrepreneur, for that alone enables the person to express himself freely. The sounding board is particularly essential when the entrepreneur has initiated the steps to walk the path of growth and modernisation of his firm. In managing the pangs of growth, that is, while devising systems of work, assessing existing staff, inducting new persons, taking decisions regarding asset expansion and sales planning, he definitely profits from another's point of view and a voice of dissent. For, unlike filing of a return to a government office, decisions taken in these matters are of long-term and serious implications. The more he deliberates on them the better; the more they are critically analysed for him by some one, better still.

While running your tight ship you may pretend to be omniscient. May be you have opened the engine several times for minor repairs and know it thoroughly. May be you are a tough sailor who can work as hard and as well as any deck-hand. But surely someone who can read the compass as well as you think you do can only help you navigate the ship better.

Your Response

We want to hear from you!

The details you provide here will help us produce more meaningful books for you and get them to you faster. Kindly fill in the details, cut out this page and return it to: *RESPONSE BOOKS, A division of Sage Publications India Pvt Ltd, Post Box 4215, New Delhi 110 048.*

(please print clearly)
Name: _____ Designation: _____

Address:
Home: _____ Office: _____

_____ _____

_____ _____

How did you come to hear about this book?

☐ Brochure/catalog ☐ Recommended by a friend/colleague/teacher/peer

☐ Advertisement in _____ ☐ Other (please elaborate)

☐ Bookstore

How did you obtain this book?

☐ Bought it at a bookstore ☐ Borrowed it
☐ Checked it out of the library ☐ Ordered it directly
☐ Other

What do you think of this book?
(please state your views frankly—use an extra sheet if necessary)

_____

_____

What are your areas of interest? (please indicate broad disciplines)

_____

_____

Would you like your name to be included in our mailing list?

☐ No
☐ Yes, enter my home address
☐ Yes, enter my office address